The Design Politics of the Passport

The Design Politics of the Passport

Materiality, Immobility, and Dissent

Mahmoud Keshavarz

BLOOMSBURY VISUAL ARTS
LONDON • NEW YORK • OXFORD • NEW DELHI • SYDNEY

BLOOMSBURY VISUAL ARTS
Bloomsbury Publishing Plc
50 Bedford Square, London, WC1B 3DP, UK
1385 Broadway, New York, NY 10018, USA

BLOOMSBURY, BLOOMSBURY VISUAL ARTS and the
Diana logo are trademarks of Bloomsbury Publishing Plc

First published in Great Britain 2019
Paperback edition published 2020

For legal purposes the Acknowledgments on p. xi
constitute an extension of this copyright page.

Cover design: Avni Patel
Cover image © Shutterstock

A catalogue record for this book is available from the British Library.

A catalog record for this book is available from the Library of Congress.

ISBN: HB: 978-1-4742-8939-9
          PB: 978-1-3501-4308-1
        ePDF: 978-1-4742-8937-5
        ePub: 978-1-4742-8938-2

Typeset by Integra Software Services Pvt. Ltd.

To find out more about our authors and books visit www.bloomsbury.com
and sign up for our newsletters.

All the birds that followed my palm

To the door of the distant airport

All the wheatfields

All the prisons

All the white tombstones

All the barbed boundaries

All the waving handkerchiefs

All the eyes

were with me,

But they dropped them from my passport

Mahmoud Darwish

Contents

List of Figures

Acknowledgments

I am deeply grateful to those who shared their stories, histories, and struggles of border crossings and transgressing with me during these years: undocumented migrants, asylum seekers, forgers, and migration brokers. I am indebted to the companionship of Shahram Khosravi, a friend, teacher, colleague, and brilliant scholar. Without Shahram and his inspiring work, I would have not started this project in the first place. I am grateful to those who I met during my time as a PhD candidate at Malmö University, which eventually led to this book; to Eric Snodgrass, Maria Hellström Reimer, Susan Kozel, Christina Zetterlund, Ramia Mazé, Erling Björgvinsson, Jacek Smolicki, Anna Lundberg, Berndt Clavier, Åsa Ståhl, Kristina Lindström, Temi Odumosu, Carina Listerborn, Johan Redström, William Walters, Mathilda Tham, Christine M. Jacobsen, Oscar Hemer, and Andrew Morrison. Thank you all for your insightful comments, engagements with the work, and sharp criticism. Thanks to Parsons School of Design, the New School, which hosted me in spring 2014. The idea of turning my messy notes and unfinished lines of thought to a book on passport came to mind while being there. Victoria Hattam, Miriam Ticktin, and most importantly Clive Dilnot were crucial in this sense. I am grateful to Rebecca Barden at Bloomsbury who believed in this project and convinced me to publish this book; to the Department of Design at Linnaeus University and particularly Ola Ståhl; to the School of Design and Craft (HDK), University of Gothenburg, and particularly Erling Björgvinsson. Both spaces provided me with a short but important and much needed time for working on this manuscript. The final stages on working with this book were the beginning of my work at the Engaging Vulnerability Research Program at Uppsala University. I would like to thank all the members of the program and particularly Don Kulick, Mats Hyvönen, Sverker Finnström, Maria Karlsson, Sharon Rider, Erik Hallstensson, and Karl Ekeman for their critical comments on the final manuscript of this book. Thanks to all the members of Decolonizing Design for your struggles, laughter, frustrations, as well as our inspiring and challenging collective project:

Luiza Prado, Pedro Oliveira, Ece Canlı, Danah Abdulla, Ahmed Ansari, Matt Kiem, and Tristan Schultz. My deepest gratitude goes to my lifelong friend Amin Parsa for never-ending cups of tea and discussion over this project and many others no matter how far, how close. My family in Iran has always been a source of joy, support, and learning. I thank you all. To Sofi, my lifetime comrade and Levi who does not have a passport yet: without you, your love, and courage, not only the presence of this book would be in question but the life in itself would be worthless.

Portions of this book appeared previously in two articles published in *Design Philosophy Papers* 2015, Vol. 13 (2) and 2016, Vol. 14 (1–2) and a chapter in *Tricky Design: Ethics of Things*. These portions are reproduced here with the permission of Taylor and Francis as well as Bloomsbury.

Introduction: Design, Politics, and the Mobility Regime

The freedom of movement [...] is not the end purpose of politics, that is, something that can be achieved by political means. It is rather the substance and meaning of all things political.

Hannah Arendt

It was autumn 2012. A gloomy afternoon approached as the clouds loomed over the sky of Malmö, a city located in south of Sweden. I was sitting in the kitchen of my apartment listening to Nemat, a young, calm, slim boy from Afghanistan. I had known him for six months by this point. His family had fled the war in Afghanistan in the 1980s and had migrated to Iran. He was born and raised there and resided in Tehran legally until he was six years old. Then the authorities refused to prolong their permit. The family had to stay in Tehran undocumented, since going back to Afghanistan in 2002 was not an option. The country was just occupied by US forces. The consequences of being undocumented meant living in constant fear of deportation and thus being subject to exploitation at work, school, and in everyday encounters in Iranian society. When Nemat was 12 he had to begin working—in sectors including construction, tailoring, and household production workshops—to help the family bear the high costs of an undocumented life. When he was 15 the family decided to go back to Afghanistan as their situation in Iran was becoming worse. However, things did not work in their hometown of Ghazni as they had imagined. Afghanistan, a playground for different Western military forces since the 1970s, was too dangerous to live a life. After a few months, they decided to go back to Iran. They did not have a passport or a visa and, even if they had wanted to get one, it was an impossible task. The family had to travel separately as crossing altogether would have hindered their chances of crossing. Nemat crossed the border to Pakistan first with the help of smugglers and from there he hid in a Nissan pickup truck to cross the border to Iran, where he faced shooting from the Iranian border guards who, together with the international community, consider that specific border as a battlefield for the "war" on drug trafficking. Back in Tehran and reunited with his family within a few months, Nemat decided to leave Iran for Europe as he had no place, neither in Afghanistan nor Iran. The main problem, however was acquiring a proper passport, or a "right" passport as he put it. Without one, Nemat had no place in the world. He was not given a passport at birth and his possibilities to obtain one was incredibly limited—despite the fact that he worked twelve hours per day; that he and his family contributed to the Iranian economy through their devaluated labor, and that they refused to engage in any war in their home country. "Why did you not get an Afghan passport?" I asked him. "What would I do with that? There is no use in it!" Nemat decided to take the matter into his own hands and obtain a passport that could guarantee him a place in the world, a place to live, to make, to dream. That was when his long journey of border transgressing outside of Iran started.

During the last seven years, I have listened to the stories of many undocumented migrants and border transgressors who have had different experiences of how the lack of a passport, not having a good passport, carrying a forged passport, or waiting to be granted a proper passport have shaped their conditions and their options of mobility and residence. Mundane, instrumental, and sometimes not even at stake for the privileged population of the world, namely, white middle-class citizens of the Global North, a passport tends to be directly embedded in the lives of the majority of the world's population: most prominently in the lived experiences of stateless refugees, undocumented migrants, and border transgressors, as well as working-class citizens of the Global South. To turn the passport into an object of thought stems from these non-privileged lived experiences.

In this book, I explore how the ability to move across territories is historically and contemporarily designed and commodified by following the emergence, development, and escalating uses of passports. By highlighting how the passport designs the conditions of being, moving, and residing in the world beyond the "actual" design of the passport, I aim to weave together stories of how mobilities, and more importantly immobilities, are organized through specific designed objects. Moreover, I intend to trace how mobilities are distributed unevenly and asymmetrically across various spaces by intentional as well as contingent actions and decisions.

This book argues that the passport is not neutral but a real and powerful device with its own specific history, design, and politics, mediating moments through which socially constructed power relations can be enacted and performed. Ethnicity, gender, and class come to interact, intersect, and produce inequalities through how passports work in various situations. Passports are material evidence of exercising discrimination. Passports circumvent abstract discussions of power in academia and bring to the fore stories of power relations at their sites of production, as well as in their spaces of circulation and consumption. This book explores the capacities and incapacities of the passport in granting an individual the possibility of crossing a border and thereby granting them the ability to claim the right to movement. This is to say that such an apparently simple and thin artifact is capable of helping to trace the politics of mobility in particular, as well as politics more generally. Passports thus can be thought of as instances in which the relations, contradictions, convergences, and intersections of design and politics collide. In international relations, a passport is frequently defined as a booklet issued by a national government that identifies its bearer as a citizen of that country, with permission to travel abroad and return under the home nation's protection. When traced back historically, through its capacities, and in relation to how design and politics operate, passports reveal various aspects of design as an activity that participates in the manipulation of the world, regardless of its initial and actual intentions.

The Politics of Design and the Design of Politics

While this book is primarily about passports as objects or devices, it is also about the politics that generate the design and use of the passport, as well as the politics generated *by* the design of the passport. In this sense, it is an intervention in how *the politics of design* and *the design of politics* can be explored through objects. These two approaches to understanding the relations between design and politics may help further expand on the complexities and ambiguity involved in questions of design and politics that have been addressed previously by design scholars from different perspectives.[1]

The politics of design can be thought of as relations that prescribe in advance what will and will not count as design, which order what is regulated and possible to regulate by those acts described as design practices. The politics of design is about ordering, devising, and distributing regulated and regulatable material practices. The politics of design defines who is to be called designer, and how one is qualified to talk about design; who understands the language of design and who is allowed to expand the language; who is making constructive criticism and who is foreign to it. What kind of designer can one become in such a world where the limits and meanings of the role are set out in advance? What happens when one has no place in the established regulation of the practice?[2] Much of this type of politics is produced historically and discursively, but it is also produced materially through diverse economic and intellectual practices derived from institutions in higher education; museums; the cultural, economic, and industrial sectors of government as well as commercial corporates, galleries, and design magazines (Forty 1995; Attfield 2000).

In the aftermath of Brexit, *Deezen*, a design blog, announced a passport design competition for "designs that present a positive vision of the post-Brexit UK to the world, and that represent all its citizens." The banality of such a call in washing away the politics inherited through the Brexit vote, as well as ignoring the histories and complexities of passports, by treating them only as a symbol representing a nation-state, is not a surprise. Previously, a new design for the Norwegian passport had won several awards for its "Nordic touch." Entitled "Norwegian Landscape" this entry won the contest run by the government due to the fact that "it both illustrates the Norwegian identity and makes sure the passport will be viewed as a document of high value" according to the judges (Howarth 2014). In these trivial, but very common, instances of "passport design," questions concerning who has the authority to decide upon "the Norwegian identity" and perhaps how the designer(s), and consequently their design, enforce a particular Norwegian identity are not addressed. Moreover, the design of the passport is considered only in relation to its graphic reality, representational capacity, and its symbolic values—thus its designers will be only those graphic designers giving a visual language to its interface. Here a specific politics of design in relation to the passport is enacted, which argues that the only relation between the passport and its design is the way it looks visually, at surface level, omitting the relations and forces that a passport designs through its interactions with humans. Design thus is seen as a one-way process that can be inscribed into an object by those who see themselves as professional designers.

The design of politics on the other hand can be thought of as the materialities produced by different human and non-human actors that generate different conditions for certain politics to emerge. In other words, how materials produce possibilities, not necessary by the virtue of being made, but by being transformed intentionally by humans from one thing to another—wood becoming table—as well as how they produce impossibilities for certain bodies to move, inhabit, and act in particular moments and places.

In the eyes of the public, perhaps one of the most recent indicative examples of the way the design of politics operates are the spikes or other material obstacles deterring the possibility of sleeping for homeless persons in certain areas of various cities. While these are explicit cases of using material means to regulate an order of things—or in the words of designers or city authorities prevent "vandalism"—they do not tell us much about the complex forces and relations involved in issues of design and politics beyond that of aggressive, hostile, and obvious instrumental uses of design. By highlighting this particular example as the exclusively violent one, we tend to see design as a neutral and passive instrument that can be the carrier of "good" or "bad" ideologies and intentions. However in this book, by examining the passport and its specific design, I argue the opposite: that because design always entails an imagination of certain persons, ideologies, arguments, positions, and privileges being realized in the materiality of the world, design inevitably produces specific politics of life and living. These spikes have existed for a long time in other forms in train stations, on city clocks, and in other urban spaces to limit areas for birds to land. By reducing questions of design of politics to exceptional cases of violence against humans instrumentalized through design, we run the risk of forgetting the less explicit, less obvious aggression that resides in any operating design actions. To recognize them and to act upon them, a political understanding of design and a material understanding of politics are urgently needed, which would (i) situate design as a political activity, and (ii) include matters of reworking the material conditions and possibilities of the world in our conception of "the political."

For this reason, I use the term "design politics" throughout this book to refer to the complex set of mutual relations that are the politics of design and the design of politics. In other words, this book throughout is an exploration of the concept of design politics, of what design politics, not only as a concept but also a series of practices, entails through examining the passport, its histories, its designing, and its transformations and reappropriations.

Thus, *the design politics of the passport* is about the politics produced by the material existence of passports historically and temporarily as much as the politics that drives their graphic reality. In this sense, the term "design" in this book is used in a complex and broad sense, but this does not necessarily make this a vague usage. To discuss the design of politics and the politics of design in a situated and concrete fashion, in relation to how the passport operates locally and globally, I use three meanings of the term "design." While slightly different in what they do and generate, these usages nonetheless overlap and exist in every designed situation: (i) the designed thing (the passport); (ii) the activity of designing (the different practices, situations, and contexts involved in designing passports, technologically, bureaucratically, and materially); and (iii) the actions flowing from the designed thing and the activity of designing: what I call in Chapter 4 "passporting," that is how passports design certain conditions of mobility and normalize certain bodies as being legal and others as semi-legal or illegal. This understanding of design comes from an ontological perspective. Such a perspective argues that human beings design their relations to the world and the future, as well as the possibilities to act in the present and future through designed objects, environments, services, and systems (Willis 2006). In summary, through making a world possible by artifacts and artifactual relations, human beings remake the world constantly, and consequently into an artificial horizon (Dilnot 2014). However, such a designed world is not passive and constantly kicks back; it "acts back on us and designs us" (Willis 2006: 70).

Following this, design in this book is understood as and in relation to the material practices generated by state and non-state actors in their promotion and production of a certain politics of movement. This is regardless of whether or not those material practices involved in politics of movement are seen or considered as design by design institutions and discourses. These political situations in return are considered as design or acts of designing that open up but also limit certain modes of being, moving and acting in the world. In this sense, by developing the concept of design politics this book expands the notion of the politics of design and the design of politics through the artifact of the passport, its generative practices, and the environments to which it gives shape. Overall, by thinking of passports in such an expanded manner and through interrogating the relations made possible by the artifice and the artifactual relations, this book goes beyond the idea of design as representation. Passports highlight the agency of design as an activity that consists not merely of designing artifacts and relations, but also of designing new environments in which new regimes of meaning-making and translations are produced. As much as these environments are socially constructed, they are materially sustained and reproduced; as much as they are real and pragmatic, they are fictional and illusionary. It is in this context that passports should be taken more seriously and deserve an analysis of their own. Rather than as a product or a servant of border politics, a designed service provider, we should think of passports as a set of relations within design politics that configure not only our perceptions of the world but also the possibilities for intervening into those perceptions.

Beyond a Representative Device

Passports mediate experiences of moving, residing, and, consequently, acting in the world. Due to this they can be "remediated" through other forms of representations, especially in cultural and artistic works. These works, through acknowledging the brutality of the passport as a system of control, deception, and regulation, try to open this banal booklet and redirect it as an object of thinking, imagination, and memory with the hope of reworking the hegemonic narrative prescribed to them.

Amita Kumar's (2000) beautifully written book *Passport Photos* tackles various issues of identity, home, racism, and belonging through precisely those bureaucratic features that exist in passports: photos, signatures, names, sex, places of birth, and so on. Kumar's powerful account works very well to reappropriate those bureaucratic features, turning them upside down and opening them up toward other stories: in his case often stories of the wretched, the forgotten, the underclass, and the pariah.

Some cultural practices that surround passports as a mediating metaphor for identity as well as a concrete object of identification can gain another layer of meaning after they are set in circulation. Ahmad Hammoud and Malak Ghazaly's project *Passport for the Stateless* is a case in point. As part of a larger project *Stateless of the World*, Hammoud and Ghazaly have designed a passport for the stateless person, whose lack in being recognized by any state results in lacking a passport. As part of the exhibition *Cairo Now* at *Dubai Design Week*, Hammoud and Ghazaly sent their project to be shown at the exhibition, but when the passport arrived, it was signed off and every page was ripped off (Figure 1). State security considered this fictional passport of some value, which prompted them to try to invalidate it by signing off and ripping it apart.

Similarly, but in a different fashion, Khaled Jarrar's *State of Palestine* stamp project unsettles the relations between borders, authority, and passports. Part of a larger project *Live and Work in Palestine*, Jarrar designed a visa stamp for Palestine, visited a bus station in the West Bank, and asked tourists for their passports to be stamped by the visa he designed (Figure 2). We often get our passports stamped when entering a legally existing territory. Jarrar, however, does the opposite. By stamping a visa from a non-existing territory—of course non-existing in the imaginary of the international community—into the existing legal passports, he redraws a map of Palestine and performs its borders. This happens at the moment of performance of asking for the passport and stamping it, as well as through the traces of stamp left on those circulating passports. He reminds us that passports or visas are not simply products or signifiers of the borders but rather the very components that constitute border politics. They are the very material and performative practices that produce borders. While these examples, among other ones, demonstrate, expand, and unsettle what a passport is, how it operates, and how it can be rethought differently, this book avoids engagement with artistic works concerning passports. This is because these works tend to metaphorize or universalize passports, tendencies that I aim to resist throughout this book. This is not because these approaches are redundant or unhelpful, but due to the fact that this book engages with very materialized, concrete, and non-representational situations and encounters that produce and are produced by the passport.

It might be true that passports are just another material technique of border control. However, their unique emergence, transformation, and existence can illuminate the complexity of how mobility and immobility can be produced and communicated through material practices. More specifically, due to their particular materiality and technical configurations, passports are different from barbed wire, for example. While one of the most important and determining actors in development and promotion of mobility across territories as a modern phenomenon, their specific capacities in facilitating, regulating, and producing identification at any moment and place make them unique compared to other techniques of control.

Another factor that makes passports special compared to other material techniques of border control is their actual mobility due to their configuration. Compared to the majority of border techniques, which are technically fixed and bound to the geographical location of the border, passports are conceived to be mobile, to be carried. A passport that does not accompany a mobile body fails its purpose from the perspective of the issuing authority. This makes the passport a very interesting case for studying mobility and immobility as a design paradigm that shapes specific politics of movement and migration. This book aims to follow such materialized and designed relationships and shows how passports are not only representative devices of bodies, identities, and mobilities as frequently framed by states and passport authorities, as well as the majority of the scholarship in security and border studies. Through a social and material history of passports, including lived experiences and accounts of travelers without the "right" papers, as well as those who forge and fake relationships between bodies and passports, this book argues that passports produce bodies, migratory movements, and mobilities. If this argument is true, then their design is not only operative in the formation of their shape, color, and graphics, but also more broadly in how they shape interactions between bodies and the world.

Mobility Regimes: Practices, Performances, and Articulations

A passport as a specific device of bordering politics and practice acts on behalf of the border. Passports are called upon whenever or wherever the necessity of a border is felt or desired by certain states, groups, or individuals. At the same time, they have the capacity of producing borders, stretching them temporally and spatially beyond the geopolitical lines at the edge of the territories. In this sense, passports have always been a device for "delocalization of borders" (Bigo 2002; Mountz 2011), a prevailing paradigm in recent critical literature in border studies. Because they are designed to be used, asked, traded, and reused beyond the actual territorial borders, they are capable of moving borders with themselves as it will be explained in detail in Chapter 4.

This is why it is important to understand the passport as a designed artifact that not only serves states' purposeful and oppressive policies of movement in the interest of capital and national discourses, but also a device that actively directs, frames, and articulates our understanding of contemporary politics in general and of mobility regimes in particular. By the term "mobility regime" I do not mean that celebrated notion of "new mobilities" (Sheller and Urry 2006) which emerged from post-modern discourses entangled with the acceleration of globalization of the time. Such an approach to mobilities has been challenged recently by the claim that mobilities should be understood in terms of a regime, to avoid the creation of dualities and to prevent the production of a homogenous analytic lens that discusses every mobile individual due to its assumed shared condition: mobility (Glick Schiller and Salazar 2013). While following such a critique in general, this book pushes such criticism further and argues for an understanding of mobility in relation to how mundane, material, and performative small encounters and situations configure possibilities of movement vis-à-vis the claim upon the right to move. In this sense, I interpret the mobility regime through the ways in which under particular historical and material circumstances, certain practices merge into each other, forge relations, and produce "self-evident" realities in a given time such as (un)desired migratory flows.

My understanding of "the regime" comes from the ways in which Michel Foucault discusses "practices" of knowledge production within and beyond institutions (Foucault 1977, 1978, 1991) and how these practices form a regime through repetitions, acceptance, legitimization, and normalization. In other words, regimes of practices help us "to study [the] interplay between a 'code', which rules ways of doing things (how people are to be graded and examined, things and signs classified, individuals trained, etc.) and a production of true discourses which serve to found, justify and provide reasons and principles for these ways of doing things" (Foucault 1991: 79).

Those practices do not exist in isolation. They are performed historically and in relation to other practices, both material and discursive. In order to exercise power, regimes of practices need to be performed. The performance of practices reveals the performativity of sovereignty. Regimes of practices that produce conditions of immobility, in truth, perform certain forms of sovereignty, power, and statehood. In line with Judith Butler's theorization of gender as performative (1988), the state can also be understood through its "stylized repetition of acts" such as policies, customs, paperwork, and institutions. Through its practices performed by human actors—civil servants, citizens, non-citizens, and so forth—as well as non-human actors—artifacts such as passports—the state reinforces its sovereignty (Doty 1996; Weber 1998; Feldman 2005).

However, regimes of practices and their performances within the world are not just there or given. While they are planned, their performative repetitions never produce the same result but contingent outcomes that come from a series of relations. I understand these relations as "articulations." Articulation in this work refers to a "form of [...] connection that can make a unity of two different elements, under certain conditions. It is a linkage which is not necessary, determined, absolute and essential for all time" (Grossberg and Hall 1986: 144). Articulation is not merely discursive or ideological; it is embedded in the historical conditions and material practices in which it happens. Stuart Hall (1996) argues that any articulation is always already materially and historically embedded. In his famous essay on race and uneven development in the context of the apartheid regime in South Africa, Hall explains such embeddedness as "tendential combinations" that are "not prescribed in the fully determinist sense" but are nevertheless "'preferred' combinations sedimented and solidified by real historical development over time" (330).

For instance, one of the most important historical forces that have shaped the contemporary mobility regime to a great degree is colonialism. Scholars working in fields other than design have powerfully evinced how concrete material practices of mobility were invented, designed, developed further, and used on a mass scale through colonialism. They show how the regulation of the movement of certain bodies and in particular the policing of migration and migration policies are extensively shaped by colonialism and its aftermath. For instance, how the violence of everyday life in colonies is organized and normalized through specific architecture, design, and development of racially divided zones, towns, streets, buildings, and institutions (Fanon 1963; Çelik 1997); or how a specific artifact such as barbed wire, designed, and produced for the specific site of agriculture moved to the sites of colonial wars, and later mass sequestration and detention (Netz 2010); or how the specific identification technique of biometrics was developed by the colonial state of South Africa (Breckenridge 2014); and how the current migration family visa is shaped by colonial legacies regulating domestic spaces in colonies (Turner 2014).

Therefore, articulation is about situating linkages that are inherited historically. It is also about the ability to connect and recognize disconnections, and the possibilities for forging new relations produced and generated within the materialities of the world, their histories, and their capacities. In this sense, the passport is one of the "material articulations" of the mobility regime. It does this through forging connections between different and dispersed technological, bureaucratic, and administrative practices, which consequently produce contradictory wholes, such as a nation or citizenship. By locating the passport as a material articulation of the mobility regime, we can situate the design of a passport as a matter of articulation, which allows us to discuss how the possibility to move and act is constantly produced through mundane design decisions in different localities and across time. Whereas the enforcement of carrying passports while crossing borders might be a top-down decision made by states, particularly in the Global North, the details of passports as a system of control are negotiated among different participants of the regime: politicians, lobbyists, security researchers, security companies, activists advocating privacy rights, graphic and interaction designers, existing technologies, protocols, standard organizations, and so on. This is why I do not attempt to find a single designer behind the passport but try to explore a regime of design practices that can be examined, opened up, and challenged through the single artifact of the passport.

This understanding of design's involvement in the politics of movement thus goes beyond a dichotomy of connection/disconnection or mobility/ immobility, and points to the complex ways in which the national and international circulation of goods, bodies, capital, and labor requires a giant political apparatus articulated through dispersed material practices to render certain circuits possible and other circuits impossible (Salter 2013). As recent scholarly works of critical border studies (Mezzadra and Neilson 2013; Nail 2016) argue, borders do not merely exclude and include. They produce a flow. Without borders the circulation of capital, labor, and wealth would not operate. Thus, borders do not regulate mobility; they produce mobility. The question, however, is what kind of mobility they produce and what type of bodies, things, and histories get to be mobile over other ones and at what and whose cost.

Up until the recent "material turn" in social sciences, most humanities scholars have only dealt with the discursive aspect of the mobility regime and migration in terms of its production, negotiation, or contestation. At the same time, design scholars have widely overlooked the active presence of design and designing as a historical and material agent in shaping the current order of mobility and immobilizing certain populations. This book puts forward a suggestion that design researchers need to study these practices from the perspective of the agency of design by recognizing the politics they generate. Moreover, it suggests that migration researchers need to pay attention not only to the materiality of the processes that render certain bodies as migrants, as legalized or illegalized travelers which has been done recently (Squire 2014; Walters 2014; Andersson 2016), but also to how these processes are designed, persuaded, and consumed. This is necessary in order to understand how the mundane and seemingly apolitical makings and details of design emerge as a distinctively economic and political activity that articulates specific mobility regimes both historically and in the present. Moreover, beyond the production and regulation of certain bodies and their abilities to move and reside at will, this will help us to examine how design practices develop spaces and conditions of normalcy, acceptability, or what design scholar Tony Fry (2015: 85) calls a "designed system of compliance." Such designed systems produce unequal, exploitative, and violent relations that are not seen or experienced as violent by hegemonic orders and ruling classes who enjoy the smoothness of mobility promised by discourses of innovation and progress.

Travelers Without the "Right" Papers

While following the existing scholarly works on the passport and expanding the themes explored previously such as the passport as a producer of the state (Torpey 2000; Robertson 2010), as a biopolitical device (Salter 2003), or as a specific European identification technique (Groebner 2007), this book approaches the passport from the perspective of those who do not own one or do not have access to one that can guarantee them equal admission into the current mobility regime.

Whereas this book focuses on a specific artifact, its material reality, and the relations it produces in different situations, it can also be thought of as a book about bodies. However, it focuses on how the design of a specific device shapes, regulates, and orientates bodies and their abilities to move. In doing so, it brings together the stories of heterogeneous travelers who are rendered a "group" by their lived experiences of their passports or lack thereof: asylum seekers, refugees, undocumented migrants, or what I chose to call "travelers without the right papers." Rather than being about highly mobile bodies as a celebrated phenomenon of globalization, or nomadic bodies as a celebrated and fetishized intellectual romanticism, this book is about those bodies being immobilized by passports and their design politics.

This research started primarily as my doctoral project on the material conditions that produce and sustain undocumentedness (Keshavarz 2016). During those years I listened to the stories of undocumented migrants, asylum seekers, and border transgressors in Sweden and in other European countries. Passports have been a particularly significant form of evidence, central in many stories and memories retold by different individuals I have met over the last seven years. What was common to all these individuals with different legal statuses in crossing borders or in residing in the territories they were located was the lack of a passport, or the lack of a "valuable" one, or a "right" visa. The stories in this book are told from the perspectives of those who have traveled and resided without the "right" paper. The term "right" here refers to two meanings of the term ironically: (i) being right in relation to the legal framework in which those papers are assessed; (ii) right in its social and political status in current international politics and geopolitics. For instance, having a Swedish passport—as I have obtained very recently—is an especially "righteous" paper in crossing international borders. However my Iranian passport is not sufficient in granting me the same freedom of movement I enjoy with my Swedish passport. This is also subject to time and changing geopolitics. A Yugoslavian red passport could get its bearer to almost all countries in the world without a visa, even during the Cold War. By 2008, however, the citizens of Bosnia-Herzegovina and Serbia could travel visa-free to only about one tenth of the world's 200 states (Jansen 2009).

According to the latest report by the United Nations High Commissioner for Refugees (UNHCR 2017), there are 68.5 million forcibly displaced people in the world. This is the highest recorded level registered by the UNHCR. Turkey, Pakistan, and Uganda are the top three on the list of hosting countries. This is opposed to a common assumption that considers Europe as the main "host-nation." At the same time, these statistics do not tell us anything about the lived experiences, struggles, and resistance of travelers without the right papers all over the world and about the conditions imposed upon them. This book thus tries to set the possibility to recognize border transgressors and travelers without the right papers as some of the foremost political narrators of our much-lauded era of globalization, mobility, democracy, and human rights, when what they do not have access to is not human rights but "the right to have rights" in the words of Hannah Arendt (1973).

To take the struggle of travelers without the right papers seriously means also to recognize the risks that such approach might entail. Beyond misrepresentation and homogenizing heterogeneous individuals and their different politics and practices, my work runs the risk of producing tools, analysis, knowledge, and materials that assist the state and other entities in their policies and regulations against those whose stories I tell. Previously, Paulo Freire (1968) has warned us—as researchers—that "the real danger lies in the risk of shifting the focus of the investigation from meaningful themes to the people themselves, thereby treating the people as objects of the investigation" (107). This runs the risk of "constructing" people and their suffering as problems to be analyzed, solved, and, consequently, given the social scientific treatment (Sayad 2004) or design solution that they "deserve." This is why I have tried to write this book in a way that focuses on specific conditions of immobility and the regimes of practices that shape those conditions as opposed to focusing on the travelers without the right papers themselves. In this sense, I do not aim to study travelers without the right papers whose presumed homogenized "culture" and "practices" can be objectified for the use of institutions that have (re)produced categories such as immigrant, refugees, and asylum seekers. I rather try to problematize specific produced, made, and articulated material realities within the conditions of immobility through re-narrating the accounts given by individuals whose lives have been conditioned by lack of a (right) passport. It is a form of co-interrogation of the materiality of borders and nation-states as a maintenance force behind such productions and articulations, from the critical standpoint of travelers without the right papers. The anthropologist Nicholas De Genova (2005) calls such interactions a form of "anti-anthropological ethnography." While stories told here are individual ones, the book seeks to bring a collective experience to the fore. This is not to say that I only put individual stories together in order to produce a homogenous category. Instead, I try to weave them together as a shared history. This is a shared history of those who are subject to the violence of the material articulations of immobility and their resistance against that violence.

One important issue in relation to those whom I retell their stories is the issue of gender. The majority of stories in this book are stories of young men or more accurately unaccompanied male minors. There are various reasons for this. I came to contact with many of the travelers without the right papers through my engagement in a local support group in Malmö. There I met mostly unaccompanied minors from Afghanistan and Somalia. However this can be thought from another perspective too: borders call as well as filter certain bodies in relation to their gender, sexuality, ethnicity, nationality, wealth, health, and class. To see, situate, and understand the bodies that "successfully" cross borders, that survive the violence of the mobility regime in order to re-narrate their lived experiences of bordering, tells us a lot about borders as various forms of "ethnosexualised frontiers" (Nagel 2003).

A few notes on the ethical issues around this book: I have changed the names of all those who shared their stories with me in this book (except when otherwise stated). I have also changed some nationalities on request. In addition, I have changed the locations of our meetings and encounters (except when otherwise stated). There are some details of practices of forgery shared by those who I interviewed that I do not reveal, as this runs the risk of revealing important techniques used by some at the time of writing. There is, however, some information in Chapter 4 about the price and types of passport available on the market that I have written about. This information is not specific and will not hinder border crossers if it is shared. Indeed, any simple online search will show the different options available, and these prices more or less match the information given by the forgers I met and interviewed.

Passport Situations

This book is structured into short blocks, organized around the moments and situations that can be called "passport situations." Passport situations can be thought of as those situations when and where a passport is important, thus rendering it as an operative as well as illuminative agent of making relationships. Moreover, situations here can also refer to the moments and localities that a passport produces. There is a binding relationship between these specific situations and passports. Passports are the producer of a condition through which passport situations emerge, and are experienced, confronted, contested, or negotiated.

To focus on situations created by passports is to avoid a universal or global history and story of the passport. As I argue for tracing the articulations of the mobility regime and call for a designerly as well as a political understanding of how they produce practices, rationalities, and persuasions, a global or universal account of these articulations is impossible. My attempt to sketch histories of the passport in the next chapter should be read in this context. More than *the* or *a* history of the passport, this chapter highlights a series of "passport situations," where different design decisions and technological practices entangle with economic and political contexts of different times, and fashion the passport as a functional product of progress and civilization.

Chapter 3 focuses on how power relations produce and are produced by passports. This is done through a non-linear move from the artificial to the political and back again; from the design of passports, to their biopolitical features, to the reverse of this; from objects, to ecologies, to bodies, and back to designed interfaces mediating experiences of immobility. This is an attempt to explore how design and politics operate internally and mutually.

Chapter 4 expands these internal operations of the design politics of passports by focusing on what I call "passporting" and its operational modes. Materialities, sensibilities, part-taking, and translating as the four main modes of passporting are discussed and analyzed. I show how the same modes that make the passport legible lay the ground for the limits and vulnerability of passporting and the mobility regime. I do so by showing how forgery uses them to obtain a degree of mobility for those who have no self-determined place in the mobility regime.

Previous works on passports as objects of analysis focus only on passports in themselves and stop the analysis at the point of production and use of passports. This runs the risk of freezing this artifact as unchangeable. From design's perspective, discussing the passport without identifying its possibilities of being remade, reappropriated, and redesigned seems incomplete. Forgery as an act of redesigning passports and the relations and situations they produce, through recognizing the very artificiality of those relations, is also an inevitable element of the passport. Without passports, forgery would not exist, and without forgery, passports would not be redesigned constantly with higher security standards. Discussing one without the other seems a half-done task from a design scholar's point of view. This is the issue tackled in Chapter 5. Through a series of interviews with forgers, this chapter frames forgery as a specific critical technical practice that sometimes teaches us about the material politics of the mobility regime better than the object of inquiry in itself.

The final chapter of this book reflects on how the study of the passport and its regimes of practice can be helpful in establishing a wider concept of design politics. It shows the vulnerability of design in its artifactual relations to the world as well as the limits of its intervention into the world. This may help to sketch out an account of what an ethics of design could entail, based on the struggles of those whose relation to the world and its possibilities of access, movement, and residence are limited and yet are negotiated by design constantly. Such an understanding of an ethics of design is concerned with recognizing the politics and history involved in (re)designing artifacts such as passports, as well as interrogating the relations and conditions that produce a world so inhabitable and open to some, yet so violent, confined, and unlivable to others, who struggle to remake and rearticulate it. This book is an attempt to emphasize such historical and political urgency in design and designing.

2

Histories

History of passports, like history of any other human-made, artificial devices, is multiple. These histories emerge from certain social, technical, economic, and political forces and plug in to other ones. A traditional historical perspective on artifacts and products would discuss *the* history based on the specific style of their designers, its associated design school or historical periods as well as the rational and linear technological progress shaping the artifact. In order to approach *histories* of the passport, the first step is to refuse to follow such a dominant pattern of design historicism. First, because a single designer behind passports does not exist; second, because histories of violence, control, and resistance through designed things cannot be merely traced through grand periods and events, rational progressivism, or the individual professional designers and crafters behind them. Instead, they can be understood by paying attention to the complexities of how different emerging forces of the time enmesh with activities of making and designing, and consequently conduct, regulate, or direct ability of certain bodies in inhabiting in and moving through the world. As such passports have no definitive origin (Mongia 1999: 201), and it is in this sense that more than *the* history of the passport, it is more productive to think of passport situations in various and complex historical contexts.

Passports in the form of papers granting the right, or sufficient means, to pass can be traced back to the birth of territories when these geo-political spaces were defined and demarcated by certain authorities, and therefore the movement of individuals between them was subject to facilitation as well as prevention. With the various shapes, functions, and productions of subjectivities that they promote, all such papers share one common thread from their earliest use right up until the present: they are usually issued by a powerful institution such as a king, a bishop, a council, a government, a state, or another such body. These institutions due to a partial or full monopoly over territories are supposed to provide access to mobility and protection during the time of absence by means of identification. This means that a king, a bishop, a government, or a queen would be able to certify that she or he knows and identifies the bearer of the paper—letter of conduct, ID card, passport, and so on—thus asking for her or his protection and the facilitation of her or his movement. Evidence of this still exists in UK passports and passports from other former colonies of the British Empire.[1] While these institutions could not and cannot control all movement, they reserved authority over access to mobility and continue to do so (Torpey 2000).

In Europe, until the fifteenth century, papers, seals, and wax panels were artifacts sustaining such authority, certifying and identifying individuals through a description of their social status. In this case, all these artifacts were devices of privilege, which provided recognition for authorities and officials. It was a form of making the privileged unique and recognizable in a positive way. Thus it was a device of identity creation. The materiality of these devices, in fact, produced certain sensibilities in the community and made some groups and individuals seen and heard more than others, simply on the basis of the privileged few carrying a wax panel in their pockets. For instance, despite what was promised as the English subject's freedom to depart in the Magna Carta, English rulers in 1381 forbade all but peers, notable merchants, and soldiers to leave the kingdom without a license. This was mostly due to the rulers being concerned that uncontrolled departure would facilitate deviation from the fate (Warneke 1996, cited in Torpey 2000).

Having the "Right" Paper

Because of developments in the production of paper, in the mid-fifteenth century these devices gradually became more encompassing and began to be used for new purposes. To this end, this required other ways of making and promoting identification. Papers indicating individual description according to the bearer's appearance were imposed as obligations by the authorities on all travelers (Groebner 2007). Thus, a new and important feature of "having the right paper" according to the regulations of the time was introduced to the act of traveling or moving.

Moreover, the introduction of new identifying papers as necessary for travel can be seen as targeting specific groups of people, that is, the poor and underclass. Such groups were specifically those suspected of having contagious diseases, being vagabonds or engaged in illicit trading, and so on. It is important to discuss the prevention of movement for such groups not only in the context of morality or social fear but also in terms of economic exploitation. For instance, Robert Castel (2003) writes that the reason for banning begging and vagabondage was that they embodied escapes from feudalism and wage labor. The laws directed against the poor were both a reaction to frequent uprisings against the feudal system and an attempt to control the mobility of labor. Similarly, Papadopoulos et al. (2008: 52) write that in France, at the end of the fourteenth century, the introduction of domestic passports in the shape of certificates, the possession of which was mandatory for any person wishing to leave their borough, was an attempt to control mobility without labor contract:

> The certificate had to detail the reason for the journey and the date of return to the area of residence. Such attempts to limit the mobility of labour evidence something of the force of flows of mobility. What is clear is that the paid labourer, working under a contract in conformity with the law, received permission to move. Thus, it is not the journey that was problematic but mobility without a labour contract, mobility which threatened the means then available to control both the level of wages and the work carried out.

According to the official documents from mid-fifteenth-century Europe, the French term *passeport*, which literally means to pass through a gate or door, was mentioned several times and was soon adopted in many other European languages such as *passaporti* in Italian, and as *passzettel* or *bassborten* in corresponding German regulations (Groebner 2007: 172). It was in the sixteenth century that every traveler had to carry a passport in order to be identified and protected. Furthermore, every traveler had to pay for such a service. This was due to the fact that traveling was still a privilege. Furthermore, such requirement would consequently regulate the mobility of the unwanted populations whose movement could be potentially dangerous in the eyes of the state.

The Danger of Moving Actors

While all these documents described a specific status of the privileged bearer as soldier, pilgrim, or traveler, declaring that she or he was separated from others and thus subject to specific protection outside the territory to which she or he belonged, two other social and ethnic groups became subject to such documents as well: beggars and Roma. The imposition of a general ban on begging came with the introduction of public support for beggars in sixteenth-century Europe, which produced a system of identification papers in order to categorize and classify them. Beggars had to wear specific badges, visible to the public and officials, which indicated that they were registered and in receipt of alms. Roma people also had to be registered and identified. Here, papers, documents, and badges were not only a rational way of categorizing and delimiting populations, but still further, an exception that had been granted for these individuals to remain in a certain territory in which any unlawful act would result in their expulsion.

The need for documents for privileged wealthy travelers to travel safely coupled with the imposition of registration of Roma and beggars further enforced the registration of migrants who had to be assessed to ensure that they were genuine Christians and not Jews. These led to a system that developed into an obsession with registering everyone and everything. From the late sixteenth and early seventeenth centuries, authorities began to register everything and everyone (Chamayou 2013). The desire to identify any actor that could move or be moved derived from a complex set of motivations. These pertained to anything from controlling people, animals, and goods in order to regulate markets, to anticipating and preventing social and political risks and avoiding "racial and sexual threats." In general this practice was about exercising power and control over things with the ability to move. It was not merely an act of disciplining criminals or potential criminals, one can say, but rather acting upon a realization that moveable actors *in general* could be dangerous.

Since governments were not able to carry out their projects of full identification and registration completely, other power relations outside the space of state governance emerged on a smaller, local level as well. For instance in Leipzig, poorer tenants living in the cheaper suburbs were called

Zettelbürger (originally *Zetteiblirger* meaning paper citizens) because they had to have paper permits stating their landlord's surety when moving inside the city (Groebner 2007: 200).

The post-revolutionary France constituted the first European state composed of "citizens" who were considered equal and not subjects ordered by the ranks determined by the court (Cole 2001). After an attempt by revolutionaries in 1789 to abolish the French royal passport laws of 1629, a new round of passport legislation was enacted in 1792. According to Gérard Noiriel (1996), the practice of the direct registration of individuals was not monopolized by states until September 20, 1792. He writes that from the moment that a government decreed the establishment of civil status (*l'état civil*), "an individual could only exist as a citizen once her or his identity had been registered by the municipal authorities, according to regulations that were the same throughout the national territory" (xviii).

All domestic and foreign travelers had to carry passports. This was done in order to prevent oppositional forces from assembling, suppressing vagrancy and crime as well as prevention of infiltration of foreign agents. While other European states did not share the same conception of citizenry as France, nonetheless they picked on the idea of passport as an effective way to control mobility, suppressing dissent and those whom they perceived to be criminal. It is crucial to state that the reintroduction of passports as an obligatory document for travelers did not continue until the present without interruption. In the last third of the nineteenth century the obligation to present passports or any identity documents for crossing borders in Europe disappeared once again. This disappearance was such that a French historian called passports at best an object of legal historical research, with no bearing on the present (Groebner 2007: 235). Passports, however, did not disappear. The practice of identification remained pervasive for poor, enslaved, and groups in society which were regarded as suspicious, such as Roma and vagabonds, and freedom of movement was achievable only for wealthier groups. In the late nineteenth century, many first-class passengers were exempted from identity checks, while craftsmen and wage laborers were required to certify their rank and status through identity papers in order to avoid punishment for vagabondage.

Knowing the Unknown at Distance

Scholars have argued that bureaucracy has particularly arisen when the mission of governments has come to be about knowing and recording individuals as much as they could (Cole 2001; Hull 2012; Gitelman 2014). In 1797, the German philosopher Johann Gottlieb Fichte argued that if a well-functioning state is desired, an apparatus for identification, recognition, and traceability of all people regardless of their status and rank is required (Fichte 2000: 257).

If the pre-fifteenth century's identification documents functioned in the presence of the privileged subject who was carrying them in the absence of the issuing authority, the new identification systems expressed the need for the presence of the authorities everywhere and at all times even when the subject of identification was not present. One can argue that the current rationalization of identification started at that point in time. Once the will to register everything and everyone was put into practice gradually from the sixteenth to the eighteenth centuries, piles of paper and stacks of information in the form of databases of individuals and central registries were born. Whereas before a letter of conduct from a king signed by his authentic hand could enable passage for its bearer, now new documents required new technologies. They had to be compared with something else. A new technique of control came to function not only on the basis of the bearer's presence, but also on her or his absence. While this is an important point, such will to registration was not put into practice internationally and completely until the twentieth century due to weak technologies of the time and bureaucratic workloads. However this proposal changed the meaning of authenticity. If the previous documents were authentic because the authentic hand of the king or bishop signed the paper, then the documents of later generations were recognized as authentic only if they were matched with official registration databases and archives. The need to establish central registries as well as issuing papers to individuals for examining her or his trustworthiness was legitimized in the words of a French jurist in order to "detect the wolves among the sheep" (Groebner 2007: 201). Similarly, Spanish jurists proposed a plan of registration titled "New regulations for the New World" in order to monitor the population of their colonies in overseas dominions. This was the beginning of modern administration or "paper knowledge" as the media scholar Lisa Gitelman puts it (2014).

The scholars and historians of modern and bureaucratic states have rigorously discussed and examined these claims and rationalizations by arguing how colonies were turned into laboratories for colonial and imperial powers to test new techniques for identification and producing knowledge based on bodily shapes and measurements of the colonized. This paved the way for racial segregation within the governed space of the empire both within and outside of national and imperial and colonial frontiers (Arendt 1973; Lake and Reynolds 2008; McKeown 2008; Breckenridge 2014). Since their emergence until today, histories of passports have been histories of never-ending attempts to bridge the gap between identity and identification practices. Such bridging entails an assumption that unknown individuals can be known at any moment and any site by capturing and recording the unique features of their bodies. While very different and unique in their own historical contexts, detailed descriptions of bodies by means of finger prints, photographs, shadow printing, retina scanning, and so on all follow such logic. In the core of this logic lies the frequent practice of deception. Bodies are seen, known, and regulated based on their capacity for deceivability facilitated by identification documents in which passports are the main one. As such, deception and identification go hand in hand. This nexus, however, is not a mere product of the emergence of territories, population growth, and more movement across territories. This nexus is a particular European and imperial practice in the name of science and modernity legitimized within colonial practices (Groebner 2007; Clancy-Smith 2012).

The Agent of Empire

Histories of passports are not histories of specific states' documents. They rather should be seen as histories of state formations and this is more evident in relation to the issuance of passports in colonial contexts. In colonized India for instance, Radhika Viyas Mongia (1999) argues that British passports issued to British subjects in Indian subcontinent, more than being documents that made certain bodies belong to the British Empire, indeed were part of formation of British Empire worldwide. Moreover, and within the spatial formation of the Empire through passports, an idea of race determined the new aspects of state formation. For instance, the Indians who were willing to migrate to Canada were required by the Canadian governor to have passports despite both India and Canada being territory of the British Empire and thus moving within those territories was considered free. Their migration was allowed if they made a continuous journey and were able to show that they have enough money to support themselves in Canada.

Mongia's exploration of passport requirements for Indian migrants to Canada is illuminating in many senses. By controlling the movement of racialized members of British India, she argues that it is not any migration, but "precisely 'raced-migration,' that generates a state monopoly over migration practices." It is such a fabrication "via the passport [that] gives us the specifically modern imbrication of the state, the nation, and race, an imbrication that produces 'race' as a 'national attribute,' codified in the state document of the passport" (528–529). Consequently, this shows that the use of passports was not a matter of state protection as frequently discussed in historiography of the state, since both Canada and India were part of the British Empire. A passport system targeted only toward Indians and mostly Sikhs proposed by Canadian governors thus was a way of racial exclusion without naming race. In this sense, passports were a significant form of technology in forming states along the race. Passports were not obvious products of nation-states; it was the control of migration by different means such as passports exercised by the empires that foregrounded the emergence of nation-states.

Another example of the formation of racial subject through passports and within the space of empire is the specific Haji Passport issued to Muslim pilgrims to Mecca (Lombardo 2016). While it was first required by the Ottoman Empire, the pilgrim passport issued by the British rulers gradually became a divisive agent of marking Hajis separately from other travelers. While standard imperial passports existed exclusively for "Indians of means and respectability" (Singha 2013: 313) to enable their travel, Haji passports, as well as specific passports issued to Indian migrants and indentured laborers to Canada, Australia, the Caribbean, Mauritius, and eastern Africa (Roy 2016), were at work to circumscribe traveling.

The outbreak of the First World War intensified the passport regime for regulation of the movement of everyone between territories. Like many other phenomena, the First World War also universalized the modern passport regime that exists today. It is shocking for many that our unquestioned passport and identification system in the modern sense is barely a century old. It was during this time that new European states and their colonies built on the principles of nationhood and ethnicity, as well as along racial divisions. Certain laws and decrees were established, often called Aliens Act(s), to track foreigners, spies, and unknown travelers in order to potentially detain and deport them. The very strong bond between the passport and nationality, country, or place of one's origin—which is in itself a modern concept—is a product of combined developments in the late nineteenth century that came alongside imperial expansions as well as directly resulting from the First World War (Groebner and Serlin 2006).

The First World War introduced a state of exception in which everyone could potentially be an enemy. A series of practices to anticipate the behavior of suspicious bodies thus needed to take place in terms of tracking, detaining, and deporting. Passports were good devices for such practices: papers that had long been around for such purposes thanks to technological progression in administrative practices.

As an example, British passports as defined in the British Nationality and Status Aliens Act 1914 (Foreign and Commonwealth Office cited in Salter 2015) were single sheets folded into eight, held together with a cardboard cover. The passport was valid for two years and sometimes had a photograph attached. Photographs had started to become part of the technology of passports but were still not reliable enough. A look at application forms for passports from the UK Foreign and Commonwealth Office and its list of required information for inclusion shows that a detailed description of bodies needed to be documented since photos could not fully represent the bearer: "Age; Height; Forehead (high, ordinary, oval, slightly receding); Eyes (colours – blue, green, brown, including grey); Nose (large, straight, roman); Mouth (straight, firm, large, ordinary, medium, thick lips); Chin (round); Colour of Hair (Brown); Complexion (Fresh, pale, peachy, dark); Face (oval, thin)."

Technologies of Racialization and Gendering

Physical descriptions and production of bodies through the act of writing represented through a document were not practices introduced only due to the inaccuracy of photographs or due to their high cost. Scholars studying histories of colonialism have discussed in long the act of detail description and visual representations of physical features of colonized bodies in scientific as well as cultural documents as pairing the bodies to immoral tendencies and debased character (Carrera 2003; Stoler 2010). In particular, Simone Browne (2012), in her studies on the surveillance of blackness, writes about how a very specific technique of recording certain enslaved bodies was an early articulation of how the body, particularly its specific features and skin, came to be understood as means of identification and tracking by the state. Looking into a specific registry called *The Book of Negros*, she locates the practice of detail description of a body in the context of mobility during the British evacuation of New York in 1783. This handwritten and leather-bound British military ledger listed 3,000 black passengers who embarked on mainly British ships bound for Canada, England, and Germany at the end of American Revolutionary War. "Passengers listed in [the book] travelled as indentured labourers to white United Empire Loyalists or as free people described in this ledger as 'on her own bottom' " (Browne 2012: 547). With inscriptions such as "scar in his forehead," "stout with 3 scars in each cheek," "blind right eye," or "lame of the left arm," each entry details the passenger's physical description, age, place of birth, and enslavement. In practice, this document was "the first government-issued document for state regulated migration between the United States and Canada that explicitly linked corporeal markers to the right to travel" (Browne 2012: 545–548). Thus, the technique of making bodies legible with the modern passport system has a history in the technologies of tracking blackness in particular and practices of identification within slavery in general.

In the application forms for British passports in 1916, the photograph is given a space but is nonetheless corroborated by physical descriptions. Space for a photograph is complemented by narrative descriptions of the nose, face, complexion, brow, eyes, and so on (Salter 2015). With the rise of photography and easier techniques of reproducibility, the attachment of an individual's photo gradually became obligatory. During this time, Alphons Bertillon, a French law enforcement officer and an expert on biometric identification, proposed the use of fingerprints for passports in order to overcome the long-standing gap between the representation of the person on paper and the actual body. By this time fingerprinting was used in the colonies of the Western imperial states and anthropometry was used in European cities (Cole 2001: 32). While both were concerned with the main issue of identifying the unknown, the former was deeply a product of economic exploitation, free labor, and enslavement, and the latter was a product of experimental science on lower classes and underclasses of Europe. These technologies were not merely new advancements and techniques to identify, record, and recapture bodies more accurately. They articulated the carriers of these documents as individuals with a fixed identity, thus removing people from their traditional social identities and status and redefining them in bureaucratic and legal categories (Roy 2016: 333) and consequently producing new groups and populations. The proposal for taking fingerprints when issuing new passports was faced with resistance in France, since it was a form of "dehumanization," linked to documenting and indexing criminals (Groebner 2007: 237) as well as the colonized populations, who in the eyes of many Europeans were not considered human. Instead, taking photographs, which was a practice in no way related to the underclass society but rather part of a bourgeois tradition of photographic portraits, was embraced in the regime of modern passports. Another visual categorization was made in passports that were produced during 1917 in France. The passports that all foreigners above the age of fifteen had to carry included the bearer's nationality, civil status, occupation, photograph, and signature. However, special color codes were also employed to mark out wage earners in agriculture and industry (Noiriel 1996).

It is important to state that the medium of photography, which became a popular and standardized technique for bridging the gap between the body, identity, and its representation in passports in the early twentieth century, was first implemented and trialed on marginal groups. For example, Eithne Luibhéid (2002) demonstrates how photography was first used for recognition of Chinese immigrant women in order to regulate their entry into the United States according to sexual politics. She argues that after the Page Law (Page Act of 1875), which was the first restrictive immigration law that prohibited the entry of immigrants to the United States from Asia who were considered "undesirable," Chinese women "were actually the first immigrant group in the United States on whom passport-like controls were tried out. In this respect, Chinese women's experiences both illuminated and facilitated key aspects of 'modern' state formation in the United States" (52). She continues that photography, as a technique capable of officially recording the body's distinctiveness and using that record to control an individual's mobility, was first used on Chinese women before any other group of immigrants, because of the "threat" of their sexuality to the United States. A photograph was attached to each woman's consular clearance, and another photograph was sent in advance of the ship, so that when the ship arrived, officials already had in their possession photographs of the women who had been approved for migration. Women who arrived without photographs or who did not match the photographs that had been sent in advance were detained and deported to Hong Kong. Through these very techniques, officials tried to ensure that if a particular woman was cleared for immigration on the basis of biographical data provided, another woman was not sent in her place. In contrast, officials did not attempt to link together specific biographies and bodies in the case of Chinese men or anyone else who immigrated at that time.

The technologies of identification such as fingerprinting, photography, and color coding with their own historical contexts and contestations both shaped passports and were shaped back by their utilization in the passport system. This reciprocal relationship emerged along racial, gendered, and class attributions. They conducted the relations of trust between the center and periphery of empires and nation-states as well as within the peripheries. These specific techniques and the ways they have been used signal an encounter with an "unshaped other" whose deceivability was in question, someone who was hard to identify, capture, and, consequently, recognize and thus was potentially a dangerous moving actor.[2]

Stateless by Passport

When passports become necessary for everyone, lack of a passport or its deprivation becomes a means of power imposition, discrimination, management, and control. Once such a material or artificial entity becomes the only way to pass or move freely among territories, its absence leads to the prevention of motion. In Italy, for instance, in August 1914, the country suspended the right of emigration for those who were obliged to do military service by annulling all passports in their possession. Another example of this is the decree of December 15, 1922, in which the newly established Soviet Union denationalized some of its subjects by invalidating their passports and consequently rendered them stateless (Torpey 2000). Later the same year, the Soviet regime began to prohibit emigration. In the United States, through a decree described as "[a]n act to prevent in time of war departure from or entry into the United States contrary to the public safety," the government promoted more restrictions on movement to and from the country. However, in 1919, a revised version of the act no longer mentioned leaving country, only entry, stating that every foreigner wishing to visit the country would have to carry a passport and a visa issued by American authorities in her or his home country (Torpey 2000). During the fragile peace of the interwar period, all of these acts with revisions, such as the American one, remained intact and became powerful instruments to regulate the movement of undesirable migrants, enemies of the law, anarchists, revolutionaries, and so on. For example, all US governments during the Cold War banned certain individuals who were suspected of involvement in communist activities or of having communist beliefs from gaining passports.

The examples of withdrawing an individual's passport or banning her or him from acquiring a passport can be seen as the very first material act of prohibiting movement, but this act can also render bodies stateless in the event that they do leave the territory. Thus, passports not only produce national populations, but also produce populations without a state.

What was introduced as a temporary contract or exception during the First World War became permanent, standardized, and institutionalized and formally entered into the domain of international relations in 1920. That year, the League of Nations held a conference on passports, the "Paris Conference on Passports & Customs Formalities and Through Tickets," the results of which were passport guidelines and a general booklet design. The conference was followed up by further conferences in 1926 and 1927 (League of Nations 2002).

As a result of the First World War and the rise of nation-states that were trying to constitute ethnically homogeneous states following detachment from many colonies, movement across the world became increasingly regulated. What became the norm after the First World War in the form of the artifact of a passport quickly gave shape to several restrictions on migration, which could be turned into practice more easily. With the process of the creation of states that identified themselves with a particular conception of ethnicity and nationality, several groups failed to be recognized as a "state's people" and, in Hannah Arendt's view (1973), were guaranteed and promised rights by an international body in the form of the League of Nations. Because "the nation had conquered the state" Arendt writes, the meaning of citizenship and protection by the state became accessible only through recognition as nationals of that state. Thus, the rights of non-nationals could be guaranteed only by a supranational body that was a by-product of the process of creating nation-states. As nation-states needed to identify who belonged to which particular nation, passports and identification papers had now become necessary for every single traveler.

The League of Nations at first resisted the systematic rise of passport making, which was a result of the First World War and violent nation-state building processes that, in turn, left many migrants stateless, producing a population called refugees. However, it finally gave up its opposition when it had to find a solution to the so-called "Russian refugee crisis" in early 1922. Since refugees, travelers without a nation, or stateless and immobile migrants failed to identify themselves according to new national regimes of recognition, the League decided to copy the practice of nation-states, and produced passports for non-nationals or refugees, thus identifying them as a new population. This product, called the "Nansen passport," would allow stateless individuals to identify themselves according to the data recorded by the supranational body of the League of Nations (Figure 3). The product was a result of an agreement between sixteen European states, which could now issue traveling documents for Russian refugees without committing to giving any citizenship rights to their bearers. The states agreed to recognize these papers as valid but at the same time, they were not required to admit their bearers. By the end of the 1920s, more than fifty governments had joined the agreement and it was considered a success. While the Nansen passport was originally made and issued in order to give limited access rights to Russian refugees, it expanded its protection to Armenians, Assyrians, and other stateless populations (Torpey 2000).

In fact, the issue of refugees in the aftermath of the Russian Revolution was managed through the invention of a new category of passports, which is the origin of the Refugee Pass or *Laissez-Passer* of today. One can argue that what created refugees as a population was not only the invention of the nation-state, but also the invention of passports as a way to recognize who belonged to which nation-state and who did not. The solution for the management of refugees was therefore a part of the system that had produced it. However practical and successful this solution was, it sustained the passport regime by producing various categories of passports, thereby legitimizing the passport itself and shifting the question from the nation-states and their practices of exclusion to practical matters of achieving the right papers according to the defined categories. In an analysis of modern refugee law, it has been argued that "[t]he beginning of international refugee law can properly be dated to the creation of the Nansen passport system" (Skran 1995: 105).

Redesigning by Stamps

On June 1, 1935, the Nazi government reintroduced a type of domestic passport known as the "work-book." Quite similar to other internal registration systems, the introduction of the work-book had the purpose of effectively registering the allocation of labor. Initially applied only to the practitioners of skilled occupations in which labor shortages existed, it quickly spread to other areas as well. Together with the registry based on all work-books issued, the little booklet documented the working life of the bearer, which included job changes, periods of unemployment, and any alleged breaches of work contracts. Through the work-book system, all Germans could theoretically be under surveillance on the basis of their labor status. "The government later extended this system, refined to keep track of changes of address, to the entire population immediately before the Second World War in the form of the 'people's registry—(Volkskartei)' " (Torpey 2000: 133). In August 1938, Reinhard Heydrich, Chief of the Reich Main Security Office and President of International Criminal Police Commission (later known as Interpol), introduced the imposition of the so-called compulsory forenames—(Zwangsname) "Israel" for Jewish males and "Sara" for Jewish females—to be listed in the people's registry. Only few months later in October, the Third Reich declared all German passports in possession of Jewish citizens invalid. It was only after their return to the hands of the authorities in order to be stamped with a red "J" sign that they were revalidated. This was in addition to the identity cards Jews were required to carry within Germany[3] (Figure 4).

Passports now entailed the capacity to reinforce restrictions that might be desired by either governmental or non-governmental actors at any moment. For example, passports made it easier for the German government to regulate and restrict migration both into Germany and to other occupied lands across Europe during the Second World War. This does not mean that the Nazis would not have been able to carry out their racist political agenda without passports. However such artifacts, which are inherently mobile, could be required to be always carried on one's person as the property of the government rather than the individual, which paved the way for the Nazis to be able to implement their ideology materially everywhere and at any moment. A body, a passport with a red "J" sign, and a checkpoint with agents controlling it could transform every corner of each street in Europe into a hostile environment for undesirable groups. A simple material setting such as this could lead to the arrest of many Jews and their deportation through such an artifact.[4] Without passports, the Nazis would have had to spend more time and money in order to track and arrest their target groups.

The possibility to redefine the validity of the passport through the act of stamping was not unique to Nazi regime of identification and control. In the modern passport regime introduced after the First World War, visas have always been a way of revalidating passports for entering into or passing through territories other than the issuing one. Visas in the form of stamps or imprints have historically been a form of redesigning the boundaries of how far a passport and its barrier can travel. While an internal side product of passports, visas perform a different function legally and politically. From the French word, *visé*, meaning to have been seen, the visa refers firstly to the authorization given by a consul to enter or pass through a country, and secondly to the stamp placed on the passport when the holder enters or leaves a foreign country. In modern usage, it refers to the pre-screening of travelers and represents a prima facie case for admission (Salter 2006). Visas indeed have extended the idea of controlling moving actors even before the travelers have moved or have arrived at the border.

Passports of the United

After the Second World War, several efforts were made, on a national level, to reduce the severity of the passport regime inherited from the interwar period. Even before the war had officially ended, Belgium and Luxembourg had exchanged notes aimed at reducing passport controls. By 1950, the Netherlands had joined this effort and nationals of the three countries were given the right to travel within these states with only a national identity card. In mid-1954, Denmark, Sweden, Norway, and Finland agreed that their nationals could travel without passports or other travel documents within these countries, and that such persons no longer needed to be in possession of a residence permit when residing in a Scandinavian country other than their own. These arrangements were extended by a 1957 convention, which provided for the elimination of passport controls at the internal frontiers of these Scandinavian countries (which thus implicitly extended the freedom of movement to non-nationals traveling within these countries). These agreements had wider influence, encouraging the Tourism Committee of the Organization for European Economic Cooperation (forerunner of the OECD) to conclude "that the final goal, the pure and simple abolition of passports, is not merely an utopian aim" (Torpey 2000: 68).

In the interim, those who were advocating for more liberalized movement proposed the creation of a European passport as a practical and symbolic means for creating a unified continent. During the 1950s, however, European national states showed their skepticism toward this proposal by stating that they were not yet ready for such change but preferred to see a standardization of national passports across Europe. Today, the common understanding of the European passport regime is a passport-less border crossing through the area called Schengen. However, many countries nevertheless recommend that their citizens carry their passports even when traveling within Europe.

At present, citizens of certain countries that have signed agreements such as Schengen, the Economic Community of West African States, and the Union of South American Nations on freedom of movement can cross the borders of signatory countries without a visa, but simply with a valid passport or national ID card. Various visa-waiver programs are at work between various countries. Nevertheless, passports are still the main devices for moving across borders.

Without a passport, one loses one's legal status in territories that are not one's national territory. A stateless or undocumented person, however, has no passport and thus no legal status regardless of where she or he resides.

There are various categories of passport, covering various individuals and populations. If an individual fails to obtain any of those types, they are officially rendered a person without any civil rights. Among these are regular passports, which are the most frequently issued booklet that any citizen of a recognized government might have the possibility of obtaining. Diplomatic passports are passports issued for governmental actors traveling for specifically government-oriented jobs and affairs. Family passports or collective passports are another type that covers a family or a group as a whole. Emergency passports are those issued to citizens of a state who are outside their national territories and whose passports are lost or stolen. *Laissez-Passers*, though seemingly quite similar to the last category, are in fact the new generation of Nansen passports, which are issued by national governments or international bodies such as the United Nations in order to grant the right to travel to a certain person on the basis of humanitarian grounds. The Refugee Travel Document is another type of passport, which is issued by the state to a refugee who is residing in a particular state. This document is intended to grant access to travel to any country except the bearer's country of origin.

Same Technologies, Different Power

Today, passports are more or less forty-page booklets with a hard plastic cover to protect the papers inside. The papers are made of anti-counterfeit materials and are produced in the same way as monetary bills. Each passport contains information such as the first name, family name, date of birth, place of birth, sex, nationality, country of origin, in some cases the father's name, and in some cases height. A passport also includes the signature of its bearer and the issuing authority as well as a barcode, which can be scanned in order to read the passport's embedded information. It has a digital photo of the bearer attached to it, which is often authorized with laser technology. With new biometric passports, all of this information is also stored in a chipset embedded in the passport's cover, digitally locked by the issuing body. The cover usually shows the coat of arms of the state that issued the passport, as well as the name of that state in English, Spanish, or French as well as the official language of the issuing state. Some passports have particular descriptions in their final page formally asking for protection of their bearer by other states. Some passports declare that the passport is invalid for traveling to certain countries. Each page is ready to be stamped or have a visa imprinted on it. Today, passports are usually designed by authorities at the foreign ministries of countries and issued and managed by police officials; however, there are exceptions in many countries. States follow the standards offered by the International Civil Aviation Organization not as rules but as recommendations. From the early 2000s onward, more and more countries have begun to produce biometric passports in which the fingerprints of the bearer are recorded in a chipset embedded in the cover of the document. Recently, more countries have included iris pattern scans as another information system to be recorded and embedded in passports. Instead of thinking of passports as the mere product of global empire, contemporary passports are in truth the effect of a system of standards and standardizations of identification and technologies such as face recognition, iris pattern scanning, and fingerprinting (Stanton 2008). At the same time, this system of international standards and practices is not a flat one: "Various forms of pressure (diplomatic, geopolitical, economic etc.) as well as incentives (e.g., technical support) exist, and they are relayed by the wealthy states and international organizations (e.g., the International Civil Aviation Organization) for the poorer states of the world in particular to adopt more advanced and sophisticated forms of passport technology (e.g., biometric face recognition features)" (Walters and Vanderlip 2015).

While passports tend to move toward standardization, sharing similar technologies and technological components owned by one or two multinational corporations, nonetheless, they do not share the same validity. They do not give the same power over mobility to their bearers. Henley & Partners is a law and citizenship consultancy firm that introduces itself as "a global leader in residence and citizenship planning." They use their resources to analyze and compare passports, in terms of which passports provide optimal freedom of movement in order to offer various programs of citizenship by investment to wealthy populations. The most recent passport index produced by Henley & Partners shows that while countries such as Finland, Sweden, the UK, Denmark, Germany, the United States, and Luxembourg occupy the first rank of those whose passport holders enjoy the most freedom of movement, Pakistan, Somalia, Iraq, and Afghanistan are among those whose citizens have the least or, essentially, no freedom of movement whatsoever. The relative value of different passports is naturally accompanied by visa regimes. The more useless the passport is, as it was called by many Afghan undocumented people I met, the less chance there is of updating it through particular visas. The map of passports produced according to the generated index of Henley & Partners clearly indicates how passports are linked to the economic, political, and colonial practices of the capital (Figure 5). It shows how the passports and their disproportional power over mobility can keep cheap and exploitable labor immobile while promoting the mobility of middle-class Western consumers as new global citizens.

*

The episodes in this chapter on histories of passports were mostly based on how different technologies are introduced into a device and produce certain limitations and possibilities over bodies and their movements. Grégoire Chamayou (2013), on his reading of Fichte as a philosopher of the police, argues:

> if the police could be reduced to a single principle or formula, it would end with a question mark. It would be a simple and implacable question: 'Who are you?' What defines the police, what gives it its ultimate essence is this interpellation, this perfectly concrete operation that for us has become so familiar, of checking our identity: 'Papers please!' The passport makes it possible to respond to this injunction immediately and without ambiguity. This is its principal function as an identity on paper.

But beyond recognition, passports provide the possibility of getting hold of the bearer's body at any moment. After checking the passport and letting the bearer go, the police is sure that (2013):

> [W]hen this body I was speaking to vanishes into the crowd, by knowing his name, I will be able to find him again. Inversely, if I learn his name, by

consulting a central registry I will find a description [signalement] of the corresponding body. I will know his history, I will find his coordinates, I will find him again. Given a body, find its name. Given a name, find its body. Given a set of properties, find the name and locate the corresponding body.

Passports have transformed from a privileged letter of conduct to a strong and vital agent for production of relations between a body, its individualized description, its name, and traces of its movement. These relations have functioned through acts of associations that in specific historical and technological contexts have produced particular politics and practices of capture, regulation, and immobilization. Histories of passports are thus twofold in (i) developing technologies to identify bodies by individualizing corporal descriptions and naming them and (ii) developing techniques of recapturing the very same bodies at any moment through central registry, archiving, and indexing. Histories of passports reveal the technological desire for bridging the gap between a body and its representation, materialization, and documentation in the eyes of the state. Ultimately, this act signals the desire to monopolize and gain power of identification and capture over the bodies on the move.

3

Power

As shown by the histories of the passport in the previous chapter, it is hard to understand passports without situating them in a network of practices and regulations over the movement of all moving things. In this chapter, I first discuss the artifice and the very materiality of passports in a network of relations. This understanding of passports, which I call political ecologies, emerges from the so-called "thing turn" or "material turn." Political ecologies therefore are about the dynamic relations that are produced from various forms of articulated things. Furthermore, I focus on relations of forces and explain passports in relation to what Foucault calls "biopower," as a device producing and regulating populations. This is followed by an exploration of the technologies of power traceable in practices of writing, reading, re-writing, and re-reading produced by passports. Technologies of power are often in line with prevailing narratives of progress and innovation. I understand these technologies of power as practices developed in between spaces and on laboratory levels (Latour 1987), where scientists, engineers, entrepreneurs, designers, and researchers "know what they do; they frequently know why they do what they do; but what they don't know is what what they do does" (Foucault cited in Dreyfus and Rabinow 1982: 187). Later in the chapter I focus on an explicit design concept that is supposedly an imperative quality of passports: interaction. By situating the concept of interaction within an examination of passports, I develop a critical understanding of interaction as a domain of power and an understanding of design as an act of manipulation. Therefore, I argue that every idea of interaction should be read alongside other forces such as facilitation and manipulation.

My main argument, then, is that articulations of power by passports take various shapes, scales, forms, and configurations. They overlap, expand, extend, and move through specific spaces and times and condition the possibilities of mobility. They are design and political practices, which articulate bodies, the space, and time of their movement and action. Passports teach us that any interrogation of design politics in terms of its productions and articulations as well as its possibilities of rearticulation should be carried out through a detailed examination of various forces involved. This includes the artifice of the passport; its relation to other things in a shared environment; its capacity for producing, devising, and regulating populations and individual bodies; its capacities in making certain worlds possible while restricting others; its position in an interactive setting and the action and inaction it consequently produces; and its power that hides behind details, folds, interfaces, and techniques through a systematized articulation of technologies as given and self-evident. Again, as Foucault (1988a: 118–119) reminds us:

> The relations of power are perhaps among the best hidden things in the social body ... [our task is] to investigate what might be most hidden in the relations of power; to anchor them in the economic infrastructures; to trace them not only in their governmental forms but also in the intra-governmental or para-governmental ones; to discover them in the material play.

This chapter is thus a particular analysis of the power of passports across things, moments, encounters, situations, sites, and relations through which bodies and their assigned passports operate in a world articulated by design and designing.

Objects

Objects show their autonomy to some degree when they fail to serve the purpose that humans recognize in them; they speak back, they kick back (Heidegger 1962; Schön 1983; Barad 2007). It is important to say that such a malfunction or breakdown does not always happen in the case of interruption in continuity of tools' pragmatism but also within their "bad" design or installment, their misplacements and disappearances, and their delays in the networks of continuum. In this sense, objects are understood on their own, beyond a phenomenological approach that makes them appear within human consciousness and scientific approaches that reduce objects to mere chemical and atomical constellations (Heidegger 1962). Passports in such philosophy stand out as objects beyond the facilitation or prevention of movement conducted by humans in a given space and time. This results in two main points:

The first is that objects stand as objects even if their production discontinues, their designers are dead, or their purposes are obsolete. They continue to be in the world, either in terms of resisting other objects, giving shape to them, being affected by them or preventing other objects from changing. Passports therefore participate in the world regardless of whether they are demolished within transnational territories such as Europe, or they are unused by people who have obtained them, or they were never applied for in the first place. They occupy spaces and continue to be part of the world they inhabit regardless of their designed functions. This inhabitation, whether it is stored in a closet for several years or expired and out of use in standard systems of identification, can take us to various realities.[1] Such a reading can help us to critique the romanticism around the abolition of passports within the EU.[2] Passports have already given shape to the world, and they continue to do so regardless of the prospect of a borderless utopia. One ought to remember that at several points in time, historians have argued that at best passports would become an object of historical study, a prediction that has since proved false.

Secondly, if objects stand by themselves, this does not mean that they are isolated entities.[3] A passport is an object because it is in dialogue with other objects: papers, ink, stamps, visas, checkpoint desks, pockets, hands, fingerprints, biometric chips, other passports and so on. Passports enact their agency through their relations with other objects and continue to exist through such articulations; however, they reveal themselves to us—those who have one in their possession—when we decide to book a last-minute ticket and realize that our passport expires in less than six months. An expired passport has to be handed to its maker to be penetrated by another object (in order to be punched, cut, etc.). In return, the punched passport is given back together with a new one. I assume that it is the case with many of us that we do not throw away our hole-punched, out-of-use, expired passports and continue to keep them in our closets, our drawers. We keep them regardless of their legal value, as a symbolic or practical archive of collected visas and stamps.

In the previous chapter, it was said that passports as an artifact were made in response to other materially made artifacts such as checkpoints and identification databases. It is never certain which one came first and it may not even be very important. The point is that passports, in order to be performed, have to be set in a series of relations and interactions. The positions of passports in relation to other things and humans might produce unexpected results. Today, "governmental technologies assemble scientific knowledge, technical apparatuses, anthropological assumptions, and architectural forms in strategic ways to configure relations of conduct. The implementation of illiberal governmental measures depends on material devices such as passports, databases, and checkpoints" (Opitz 2010: 104). This is how the securitization of things and humans can be read through a political ecology that can normalize or allow for the reintroduction of previously banned practices, such as torture in the form of a "technology of intelligence gathering" in the "war on terror" (Krasmann 2010) or in the form of public debate on depriving the citizens suspected of being involved in extremist Islamic organizations from their passports (Kappor and Narkowicz 2017).

Political Ecologies

Passports, while articulating certain relations and positions, are also part of an articulation. In fact, they are already within an articulation. In this regard, they have their own power beyond how they are perceived, or that for which they are designed. This is what Jane Bennett (2004: 353–354) would call "thing-power":

> The relevant point for thinking about thing-power is this: a material body always resides within some assemblage or other, and its thing-power *is a function of that grouping*. A thing has power by virtue of its operating *in conjunction* with other things.

This can be called the political ecology of passports. Ecology means here, of course, that things are in a dynamic network of relations. In the global system of passports and visa control, being part of an articulation might produce an uncertainty that is often desired by power, a type of uncertainty that targets so-called minorities the most. One instance of such uncertainty is in fact a result of algorithms produced through interactions between identification software and data-readable machines. Spivak (Spivak and Gunew 1990: 65) gives an account of what happened to her while planning to go from London to Canada:

> I was supposed to take the airplane from Heathrow on Sunday. Air Canada says to me: "we can't accept you." I said: "why?" and she said: "You need a visa to go to Canada." I said: "look here, I am the same person, the same passport ... " Indian cultural identity right? But you become different. When it is from London, Indians can very well want to jump ship to Canada; I need a visa to travel from London to Canada on the same passport, but not from the United States. To cut a long story short, [...] I had to stay another day, and telephone Canada and tell them that I could not give my seminar. I said to the woman finally before I left, in some bitterness: "Just let me tell you one small thing: Don't say 'we can't accept you' that sounds very bad from one human being to another; next time you should say: 'The regulations are against it'; then we are both victims."

It is the set of articulations and congregation of machine-readable passports and airline information systems mapped into the route from London to Canada that caused Spivak to be unable to board her flight. The same articulations, however, would have permitted the same Spivak with the same passport and same airline to fly from the United States to Canada without any problem (Salter 2015). This is how scattered items of data are articulated through a politics of probability in which judgments can be made by the suggestions offered by the security software. These "judgments" of the match analysts are made possible only by the algorithmic risk models already written by mathematicians, software designers, and computer scientists. These practitioners "'work out the best set of rules' governing the links between otherwise scattered items of data," writes Louise Amoore (2011: 64). In her work, she discusses how contemporary borders within global and data-driven systems are performed through the associations made by a combination of the state, commercial authorities, bodies, money, data, and things that dwell together in the border landscape. Passports as one such global and standardized system are thus artifactually not as fixed and solid as they may appear. They perform in articulation with other actors. These rules and codes of algorithmic models are not quite "rules" *per se*, rather a quite situated performance of codes, passports, bodies, airports, airline companies, and recent credit card purchases. They produce one risk effect on one day, at one particular airport and on one specific route, at one moment in time and quite another risk effect in other instances (2011: 64).

Passports therefore enact politics in various ways by having "scripts" (Latour 1992) embodied in them. These scripts can be seen and read, for example, from the positions different passports occupy in the ranking index of the mobility regime. Some passports require more thorough checks, whereas other passports need only a brief glance. The script of passports is always enacted in relation to other actors in the network and produces different realities and facts. This enables us to understand the script beyond the mere objectification of its inherent social and political conditions. This script could be seen as the trace left by human agency once the artifact was made, but, as shown, the script in the case of passports can change over time through its interrelation and interaction with other things, places, and humans. The politics of passports, here, can therefore be understood in "its political potential [that] resides in its ability to induce a greater sense of interconnectedness between humanity and nonhumanity" (Bennett 2004: 367).

The made or physical inscriptions are different from performative and socio-technical ones. The "socio-technical inscriptions" are those that are in between lines, spaces, and times of physical inscriptions (Akrich 1992). An artifact such as the passport does not promote explicit or physical inscription; rather, it practices, hunts, fixes, and demarcates its bearer through its socio-technical, implicit, and internal inscriptions that are often invisible to bearers but visible to makers. The designs of passports do not tell us anything about the right to freedom of movement. They do not contain the list of countries the bearers can enter without trouble. They are very abstract, despite having almost forty pages. The physical inscriptions of passports promise their transparency by bridging the gap between the bodies of their bearers and their material actualizations through biometric data, photos, names, barcodes, numbers, and so on. However, such never-ending bridging avoids the transparency of socio-technical or internal inscriptions.

Many of us—who, through privilege, use passports to cross borders—often experience standing in front of a passport check desk where officers, after sweeping our passports into their computers' reading slots, or just keeping them close enough to their RFID (Radio Frequency Identification Device) reader, stare at their monitors, which look dark to us as if they were turned off but in fact show reams of information about our various exits and entrances, our biometric data according to the latest changes in the law, our recent credit card purchases, and the airplane seats we have selected and so on. One example of such articulation of codes, practices and behaviors running through algorithmic models may thus read:

> If past travel to Pakistan and flight paid by a third party, then risk score of ***; if paid ticket in cash and this meal choice on this flight route, then secondary   checks against ***; if two tickets paid on one credit card and seated not together, then specify this risk level. (Amoore 2011: 64)

Passports are designed in a way that inscribes only the physical inscription and in turn intentionally eludes internal and socio-technical inscriptions.

Another useful reading of the political ecology of passports can be found in the idea of the abolition of passports within the EU for European citizens. It has often been introduced as a successful policy and can even be considered a determining factor for the European Union receiving the Nobel Peace Prize in 2012. The abolition of the requirement for passports within the EU, however, is not an isolated successful policy. In order to pave the way for such regulation, other actions were required elsewhere. To make this happen, attention was paid to the external borders of Europe. "Fortress Europe" was the other side of the abolition of passports in Europe. In order to develop one notion of freedom of movement, the EU needed to make passports and visa requirements stricter and more difficult to obtain on its shores (Bigo and Guild 2005). Peter Sloterdijk's works on "spheres" (2011) make a strong case that air is something that has been made "explicit"; air has been reconfigured as a result of twentieth-century technological advancements mostly through airborne terrorism and designed interior ventilations (2009). In line with his arguments, EU border politics can be seen as some sort of air conditioning system, whereby the ventilation of one environment entails the pollution of another. The EU, with its policies toward the abolition of passports for its citizens, can be seen as a privileged air-conditioned zone in which the pollution of its sides and outsides is inevitable. Consequently, the prevention of movement from the so-called polluted environments to the clean-kept environments with the help of the artificial infrastructures—visa and passports regulations—can be applied to the individuals and species inhabiting "there."[4] The population that inhabit such polluted environments can be seen as threat to the privileged zones and discourses of dust and dirt become enacted discursively and practically. In *Purity and Danger*, Mary Douglas (1966) discusses how making distinctions between purity and impurity can be used as a mechanism for sustaining existing social structures. Undocumented migrants and refugees are seen as polluted and polluting (Malkki 1995) because perhaps they are the by-products of nation-building processes, citizenship apparatuses, and exclusive freedoms of movement.[5] The regional abolition of the passport system, while the idea of the nation-state remains the dominant way of organizing international relations and political realities, calls for another system. One product asks for another to be completed and cannot stand on its own. EU passports would be meaningless if the visa regulations for European countries had remained the same as before. One artificial structure leads to other structures in which social and political fabrications are produced.[6]

Political ecologies of passports tell us that passports always already perform and interact within a network of relations and practices. To put it simply, they articulate possibilities while they are themselves a part of ongoing articulations in the world.

Bodies

Passports regulate bodies. They do this by granting access for certain bodies and not others, or making access difficult, more time consuming or expensive for some and not others, through the introduction of other supplementary systems such as visas, interviews at embassies, and requirements of proof of stable finances. In this sense, passports, visa regimes, stamps, waiting lines outside embassies for visa interviews (Jansen 2009), and border agents are at work in order to define the space and time of access. Tanya Titchkosky (2011) has observed that access should not be understood simply as a procedural bureaucratic matter, but as being about how spaces are experienced and lived as oriented toward bodies and their capacities and incapacities. Passports are therefore part of a regulatory regime that identifies some bodies as space shapers and some as "space invaders" (Puwar 2003) and consequently regulate the speed of their access. That is why the US Department of Homeland Security, which was created in response to the September 11 attacks, sorts and regulates bodies in their databases into low-risk and high-risk travelers, with the definitions of these two categories subject to change over time.

Passports document, archive, process, read, and write bodies in various spaces and times. Whereas historically the letters of conduct or privileged passports were a type of material attachment to facilitate the movement of individual bodies over territories in an easier and more feasible way, today passports have become the main body. Now, our bodies and fingerprints, our retina patterns, faces, and hand measurements are attached to passports. It is often the passport's authenticity that is checked and compared to our body and not vice versa. In the accounts of many travelers without the "right" papers I met, in moments of intended border crossing, the border guards were mostly concerned with the authenticity of the passport and not with its authentic relation to the represented body.

At the same time, it is obvious that passports are created according to our bodies. Passports are the most widely produced circulating artifacts that carry our biometric data, unique to our bodies. They are materialized in the form of chipsets embedded in the passports' covers. However, a paradox exists here. While passports are highly individualized and personalized documents that are highly codified according to our bodies uniquely, they evince universally our nationalities and our right to be protected by our state—if we have one. Passports thus shape knowledge that creates populations beyond individual bodies.

The story of Maryam Khatoon Molkara is illuminating in this sense. Maryam was the first transsexual Iranian who managed to receive a religious decree from Ayatollah Khomeini in order to undergo sex reassignment surgery (SRS) legally and legitimately.[7] She was recognized and registered at birth by the official records and society as a male named Fereydoon. After several years of struggle, she received the permission to undergo the surgery in 1987 with the approval of Ayatollah Khomeini, the highest authority in the country. Nevertheless, she was unable to undergo the actual surgery until 2003 because she was confronted with different obstacles, from the health care sector to the police and registration office who had a hard time accepting her "new" identity.⁸ While she was performing as a woman in her everyday life throughout these years, on her passport she was still a male:

> In 2001, when I had to travel to Thailand to prepare for the surgery, I had to wear men clothes after 20 years again in order to be able to leave the country with my own passport. This was a very hard and humiliating moment: a man who looks like woman, with female bodily features and face wearing suits and carrying a Samsonite handbag, created panic for many in the airport. (Molkara 2006)

A conflict between who she was and wanted to be and who the authorities wanted her to be, was articulated by her passport. Consequently, this created a spectacle in which her body was rendered the subject of public's gaze. As a result, Maryam's passport took over her body in the moment of border crossing and the performance in the airport (Figure 6).

While bodies are reduced to passports through established identification techniques, passports become bodies in the moment of border crossing. It is through passports that individuals come to know their bodies and consequently themselves as specific subjects and as internationally mobile, immobile, or partially (im)mobile subjects and bodies (Salter 2006).

Passports, in Foucault's terms, are "technologies of power" that regulate the movement of bodies. These technologies of power, which are different from disciplinary techniques of power, are a means of regulation that started to emerge in the early nineteenth century (Foucault 2003). While the seventeenth and eighteenth centuries witnessed a wide series of practices designed to produce docile bodies through disciplinary techniques, the nineteenth century was concerned with the production of bodies as populations. This required something beyond disciplinary power, namely, practices of regulation. It is worthwhile to cite Foucault (2003: 249) at length on his distinction between these two technologies of power:

> From the eighteenth century, onward (or at least the end of the eighteenth century onward) we have, then, two technologies of power which were established at different times and which were superimposed. One technique is disciplinary; it centres on the body, produces individualizing effects, and manipulates the body as a source of forces that have to be rendered both

useful and docile. And we also have a second technology which is centred not upon the body but upon life: a technology which brings together the mass effects characteristic of a population, which tries to control the series of random events that can occur in a living mass, a technology which tries to predict the probability of those events (by modifying it, if necessary), or at least to compensate for their effects. This is a technology which aims to establish a sort of homeostasis, not by training individuals, but by achieving an overall equilibrium that protects the security of the whole from internal dangers. So, a technology of drilling, as opposed to, as distinct from, a technology of security; a disciplinary technology, as distinct from a reassuring or regulatory technology. Both technologies are obviously technologies of the body, but one is a technology in which the body is individualized as an organism endowed with capacities, while the other is a technology in which bodies are replaced by general biological processes.

The population here is not at all a form of social body, but rather a dense network of relations that governments attempt to regularize. Foucault argues that in the early nineteenth century "those who inhabited in a territory no longer were understood merely as judicial subjects nor as isolated individuals whose conduct was to be shaped and disciplined, but as existing within a dense field of relations between people and people, people and things, people and events" (Rose et al. 2006: 104).

Using Foucault's arguments, one can understand passports as artifacts as well as material practices that help governments to control and manage the population. As Amoore (2011: 65) argues with reference to Foucault, the latter's depiction of security is oriented not toward the disciplinary concern to "let nothing escape," but rather to "open up and let things happen." The "space of security" for Foucault, as reported by Amoore, poses a "different sort of problem," one that must "allow circulations to take place, sifting the good and the bad, ensuring that things are always in movement." In this sense, the practices of management need to take place in various places and need to be spread out horizontally through different material articulations.

In practice, these material articulations can be understood as a "conduct of conduct" (Foucault 2014) performing upon the will and acts of moving and migrating by all those actors capable of movement. This needs to be material as well as designed in order to be effective. Conduct of conduct for the regulation of movements is not about one single artifact, rule, or practice. It needs to be a careful and thoughtful articulation of relations between possible actions and conducts. It is about the capacities that artifacts have for allowing or generating other actions beyond the defined function and use inscribed to them by the act of design. It is about how one artifact can act on behalf of the other, one action on behalf of another, and so on. It is about the third meaning of the term "design," which is to say the actions flowing from the designed thing and the activity of designing.

Take, for instance, the example of the visa regime, where those who cannot simply enter a territory with their passports need a further authorization to be added to their booklets. This authorization comes from the third state. It leaves traces in the book and requires certain practices and systems outside airports and in embassies. The visa regime allows for a delocalization of the border function so that states may engage in regulating behavior away from the physical limit of the state (Bø 1998). These interrelated and interactive material practices thus articulate an authority beyond its initial articulation. Through visas, states can perform and interact outside the state territory.

Technologies

Technologies of power, such as application forms for visas, passports, and residence permits, take shape in the form of writing and reading practices. One common reference to writing practices in relation to bodies is tattooing: attaching badges and signs and archiving and documenting them in identification databases as a means of disciplining individuals, practices that were common in medieval Europe (Torpey 2000; Groebner 2007). The tattooing of bodies in concentration and death camps has also been central to the identification and population-making practices of totalitarian regimes.

Here, however, I discuss other forms of writing and reading practices aligned with contemporary liberal discourses. If the passport has become the main body through which mobile populations are regulated, then governments need new practices of writing that are less visibly invasive than the tattooing of bodies. Codified information about bodies, the history of their movements, and their relations to other bodies and narratives are all written down in databases. As there is a materiality to coded environments (Löwgren and Stolterman 2004), reading practices always need databases in order to provide the possibility of comparison. They cannot be autonomous and always need other means and material articulations to be conducted. The need to conduct reading practices in a mobile way, since mobile individuals are involved, necessitates a new medium that can at any moment or place provides the possibility of reading and writing bodies simultaneously. Thanks to the growing publishing industry and today's digital technologies, passports can be produced inexpensively on a large scale. Considering this, what medium could possibly be better than paper? Passports appear here between the parallel practices of writing and reading of individuals and populations. Passports give their writers—states— the possibility to read the bodies attached to them in a way of their choosing. Here, new forms of knowledge appear: a whole new set of practices, skills, techniques, infrastructures, and institutions to train writers and readers of passports. Passports, then, are designed to perform the capacities to conduct such tasks.

Thus, I argue that passports exist at the point where the body and population meet and where writing and reading practices in the intertwined realms of body and population are enacted. Therefore, it is a matter of discipline, but also a matter for regularization. They can be applied to both body and population; they are "power-knowledge." It is through this that already written and known data is used to theorize and read unknown bodies (Adey 2009). This is carried out through the establishment of rationalities and norms surrounding procedures that are vital to rituals of transit spaces such as airports that are important nodes within the contemporary political economy of mobility.

While traveling to Sweden from Iran via Istanbul's Atatürk Airport, my partner, my friend, and I were in line for the last passport check before boarding. This is regularly carried out by airline staff, in order to ensure that everyone who gets on board has the right passport or visa to enter the destination, in this case Sweden, which is a Schengen State. If they fail to do so, any traveler who boards an airplane and arrives to a country without the "right" papers will be deported. In this case the airline has to pay for deportation as well as an additional fee as a punishment. Since the introduction of this rule airline staff have frequently become border guards. A young black man with a Swedish passport who was standing in front of us was asked to stand aside for a more thorough check of his passport by an officer who would most likely be an expert reader, in order to compare the authenticity of the passport and the body of its bearer with the known data. When my partner protested against this practice and asked why they did not ask her to be checked properly once again by another officer, the member of airline staff without any particular expression and without even looking at her replied: "It's a part of the normal procedure."

He did not say that it was because she looked "Swedish" or because she was visibly white and he was black, which is unknown to the international subject of Swedishness. He rather believed that such commands being shot at certain bodies was merely part of normal airport procedure. The rationalization that took place in that moment of an encounter with a momentary protest revealed and affirmed how passports contribute to the establishment of rationalities that can easily be normalized without being seen as a form of "state racism" (Foucault 2003).

Being engaged in writing and reading practices organized by governments, passports escape from top-to-bottom power forces and are set in a matrix of relations. Passports establish a series of relations between their bearers and their national state, between their bearers and the third state, and, finally, between their bearers and other individuals and actors. Passports function in terms of bodies as long as they are located in such a matrix of power relations. For instance, non-state actors can use passports in order to impose their will against the bearer's own will. This is the case with migrant workers, when employers commonly confiscate their passports in order to guarantee long-term exploitation (Berggren et al. 2007).

Another important point in discussing passports in connection to the simultaneous shaping of bodies and populations is the set of relations produced by various technologies involved in the process of issuing, validating, reading, and writing passports. The history of passports tells us how technologies of power are forced upon marginal and minor groups—historically vagabonds, Roma, Jews, refugees, and today citizens from the countries associated with so-called "state-sponsored terrorism," or so-called refugee-producing countries—as the only way to identify, detain, and possibly expulse them. It also tells us how other groups consume these technologies voluntarily, such as the privileged travelers who paid for their letters of conduct in the sixteenth and seventeenth centuries or frequent flyers who today can use iris scans instead of passports to pass quickly. These experimental techniques, however, were never tried out on a mass scale by the middle class.

Such technologies are consumed by the rich and privileged through voluntary adoption. Because they are represented to these groups as a means of ease and progress, and of smoothing the process of crossing borders, they are bought and enjoyed. However, they are forcibly imposed upon other groups. Once trialed and established as a norm and as the only "proper" way of inhabiting the world, such technologies are then introduced to all. The case of fingerprinting can be used as an interesting example. It was used to document colonized populations as well to identify criminals in the Western countries. When it was proposed as a supplementary technology for identification within the passport regime, it was faced with public protest, and the use of photography was more readily accepted.

Technologies of power can be read as mediators that establish themselves as acceptable and even necessary so that without them, the world is presented to us as less secure and thus less inhabitable. They mediate such positions through hidden or silent forms of penetration or embracing. As Peter Paul Verbeek (2005: 172) writes:

> Technological artefacts appear to be more than functional instruments. When functioning, they appear to be present for human beings in a specific way. They hide themselves in the relations between humans and world, and from their "withdrawn position" they actively shape these relations by transforming both experience and action. The way they do so involves amplification and reduction, invitation and inhibition. In this way, they co-shape both the way human beings are present in their world and the world is present for human beings.

They may at first look very invasive but when examined on both sides of the economic and social production of population and its narratives, they become less invasive, less visible, more encompassing, and ubiquitous. It is in this way that design as an activity shapes these technologies and drives them down certain pathways through defining a product, service, or system within a specific economic and social context. Design thus uses its capacities to present such technologies in a way that looks appealing, rational, desirable, and inclusive. As Keller Easterling (2005) notes, digital capitalism is sneaky, contagious, and often costumed in its material manifestations.

This is the persuasive power of design. Persuasiveness, a popular concept in interaction and computational design, could be defined as the ways technology can be used to influence people's behaviors or attitudes. Persuasive design is mainly proposed and argued for as a positive feature that can, for instance, reduce energy consumption (Ijsselsteijn et al. 2006). Those design scholars arguing for persuasiveness (Fogg 2002, 2009) often forget that what they are arguing for is the design of the "conduct of conduct," which is to say, the articulation of a series of relations for regulating the behaviors, wills, and actions of people in the interest of a certain ideology. The problem is that once articulated in the form of an artifact, these regulations do not look as if they are carried out by power relations, an ideology, or an institution from a specific context and time but simply look like innocent externalities of a designed artifact.

One feature of technologies of power is that in order to be effectively used and carried out in local circumstances, they have to operate on a global level. These localities, however, shape a form of global regime or international power-knowledge. These local practices, which legitimize themselves through a global rationality, become possible with the reproducible condition of technologies. Indeed, what makes passports valid is not the uniqueness of individuals who carries them, but rather the trace of authorities on them: "the possibility that the seal, the stamp or the signature is valid, it is because of possible reproduction that technology has made possible" (Groebner 2007: 183). The authenticity of passports does not emanate from a single original passport, but quite the opposite. It comes from the ability to be reproduced in thousands by the recognized sovereignty. If the identity of a traveler is made out of materials such as papers, signatures, seals, and chipsets, then such physical components, which make such artifacts valid, ought to be the product of reproduction techniques.

Economies

From the first days of the appearance of the passport as an obligatory attachment for any traveler, the problem of identification and authenticity has been a concern. The introduction of photographs was an attempt to bridge the gap between the body and the bearer of the papers. However, the poor quality of images and the weak techniques of attachment heightened the need for new developments in representation techniques. The use of laser technology and shadow photographs in passports was an attempt to meet such aims. Failing to breach the gap between the body and the artifact again, biometric passports or e-passports were introduced in the early 2000s. The European Union set minimum standards for all of its members to issue e-passports containing fingerprints, digital images, and other data stored both in passports and databases, categorized according to the legal status of individuals.[9] In 2010, Frontex, the European Union's border control agency,[10] commissioned a report to investigate the operational and technical security of e-passports. Their conclusion was that because e-passports have established a new regime of reading and analyzing data, a regime based on the rules of algorithmic models and associations, there is a need to establish smart gates as smart reading devices on European borders. The design of smart gates, as stated by the report (2010: 41), is simple and easily scalable:

> The [...] booth follows a straightforward design, where the traveller comes to a passport reader and when the passport is successfully read, the first door opens and passenger can be biometrically verified. When the traveller's face matches the photo in the passport, the second door opens and passenger can cross the border. The design is easily scalable and allows for an array of RAPID booths one next to another one.

These booths, however, do not look like sci-fi devices or human-like robots. They look like any other turnstile one may encounter, be it when entering subway system or a leisure center. The report adds that the booths at this moment in their experimental phase are only to serve low-risk travelers in a select few airports, and "risky" travelers or those whose bodies, passports, and databases could potentially mismatch need to be processed by human agents at the border. Smart gates as they currently exist aim to reduce the time a privileged citizen needs to spend at border control. In the use of technologies of power, design travels easily from one legitimized zone to another grey zone. Once deployment of designed devices and protocol in one environment becomes acceptable and easy to use, their use in other, ambiguous environments conceals that ambiguity and presents it as familiar, trustworthy, and "user-friendly," as the smart gates are described in the Frontex's report.

A look into the use of biometric technologies facilitated by the chipsets, which are now common in bordering practices due to the issuing of more e-passports, shows that biometric chipsets were first used and developed by credit card companies on a mass scale. In fact, the majority of biometric passports today are produced by the multinational digital security company Gemalto, which is the biggest producer of mobile phone SIM cards in the world. With €3.1 billion revenue in 2016, offices in forty-eight countries and more than 15,000 employees from 119 nationalities, Gemalto advocates that a more secure world by means of digital technologies promises freedom. This tells us how such technologies of power are not only a sovereign desire or instrument to control and regulate undesirable bodies over territories, but are also underpinned by market-driven interests that embrace every zone and individual regardless of their economies and class.

In his environmental history of barbed wire, Reveil Netz (2010) argues that barbed wire could not be used in civil wars and concentration camps before it became a cheap and profitable tool for the control of space. The profitable use of barbed wire was first established by the agricultural industry in America during the 1870s. "But it entered into human history – effectively, in the Boer War – only after its price had been pushed down through two decades of agricultural development" (Netz 2010: 231).

Barbed wire needed to be used widely; it brought profit and thus became a form of capital through its stockpiling. First, barbed wire needed to prove its functionality and profitability to human beings by preventing the mobility of cows. Only then could it be used for repression in colonial wars and, consequently, in concentration camps. Netz argues that while the Nazis would have persecuted Jews without the presence of barbed wire, "without the barbed wire ranches imprisoning Texan cows, there might have been no Auschwitz" (Netz 2010: 232). Here, he does not mean that the Holocaust would not have happened without barbed wire, but that the form the Holocaust took—the death camps—might have been different in its absence. Without barbed wire, camps would have been too expensive to build in the first place. And if the production of barbed wire had not been a profitable industry, then the creation of death camps on that scale would perhaps have been impossible.

Here, of course, barbed wire is one technology among several others that led to the production of environments such as Auschwitz. Barbed wire, however, stands for a unique technical and commercial development in this context. This should not be thought of as a cause-and-effect argument, rather as the production of a possibility through a specific material articulation that was required for later uses as well. This needs to be understood as the similarity and continuity between these events that were facilitated partly by this particular design. "They all involved, on a mass scale, control over space, which is tantamount to the prevention of motion, which is tantamount to violence" (Netz 2010: 233).

The chipset in new biometric passports works with RFID technology, meaning that data stored on them can be readable not only by an agent at borders, but also to any other machine that tries to interact with it from a particular distance while the booklet is open. These particular acts of reading, which are prescribed to the artifact of passports, are not visible or known to their bearers, simply because passports do not belong to their bearers but to the issuing authority. While old passports were filled with detailed descriptions of the bearer, of her or his name, sex, birthdate, father's name, height, weight, skin color, hair color, facial or bodily distinguishing marks, shape of mouth, nose, facial hair, ears, and so on, new passports have less descriptive information visible to bearer. Instead they carry a memory chipset, which stores dozens of pieces of information. A passport today can tell agents at the border where the passport has traveled, from which borders, and at what times.

There are many reading and writing practices embedded in passports—internal or socio-technical inscriptions—that are invisible to consumer populations. This is what design does. It gives shape to one artifact, and articulates it through the materiality of the interfaces it designs, but is unable to indicate how an artifact is situated in a complex environment of interactions and relations. Thus, design as an articulatory practice in the material world seeks to open up a space of possibility but fails to recognize that it conceals other aspects that the process of articulation always entails.

Technologies of power that are often introduced as facts produced in labs are, in truth, artifacts (Latour 2007). They are fabricated articulations between human abilities and non-human capabilities, which inhabit the very same world that labs do. Technologies of power, however, have the tendency to escape from the communality of their environment and stage themselves as something outside the actual realm, a realm that needs its own grammar and handling, its own rationale. These technologies are able to escape the discourse of power relations easily by establishing their rationale and legitimization under the guise that design offers and are then introduced and advertised as a means of achieving comfortable lives. Technologies of power are the actual material entities that are always interacting with each other in order to design, divide, partition, process, maintain certain spaces and times, and orientate bodies and things toward one direction and not another. A political understanding of technologies of power requires an understanding of power as a field of interaction. To think of technologies of power as entities involved in ongoing interactions enables us not only to critically read the effects of such interactions, but also to point out the possibility of intervening into them.

Interfaces

The fact that all things, including humans, animals, species, artifacts, artifactual relations and so on, occupy the same world means that they cannot fail to interact. History is already about interactions.

The passport situations discussed so far have taught us that the interactions between passports and our bodies and other bodies—biological or artificial—are to be understood as a set of intersections. Irma van der Ploeg (1999) has argued that biometrics transform the biological body into a machine-readable "text." She emphasizes that "the meaning and significance" of this machine-readable text is contingent on "the context," in which it is produced, and the relations that are established with other "texts." Thus, new forms of discrimination in the intersections of gender, race, and class are not only played out within a social context but also within an artificial context. It is in the interaction and intersection of socially constructed subjects with artificial machines and devices that power comes to play. Moreover, anthropologists of bureaucracy have previously shown how specific affective measures are produced through interactions between documents and their bearers in specific social relations (Jansen 2009) and "take the shape of or transform into affect and become part of their handlers in that way" (Navaro-Yashin 2007: 95).

However, it is through particular frames that a set of practices, actions, encounters, and occurrences come to be seen as interactions.[11] Any interactive setting without its frame cannot claim interactivity, for interactivity does not happen in an empty space and time. These frames can be understood as interfaces through which power relations perform and take place. The term "interface" originates within computational design, meaning a point of interaction facilitated by a graphical user interface between hardware and software. While interfaces have become an object of design since their more obvious use in personal computers (Krippendorff 2005), in his theorization of design, Gui Bonsiepe (1999) argues that the domain of design is always the domain of the interface. For Bonsiepe, "the interface is not a material object" but "the dimension for interaction between the body, tool and purposeful action" (29). This means that interfaces are designed to determine the scope of actions to be performed by an articulation of the body, product, service, and/or system in a specific situation. This definition generalizes interfaces to any activity that involves bodies, things, space, and time. While he is right in understanding the concept of interaction through the frame that makes it happen—the interface—Bonsiepe dismisses the contingency of the performativity of interfaces. The performativity of the interface means that the interface cannot guarantee that its designed functions will always be achieved, because they are situated in a matrix of relations and they in themselves produce relations in which the envisioned interaction is one among many. While the term "interface" tends to convey an image of two-sided articulation between artifacts and bodies, they are more complex. Their multiplicities contain within them many different interests, relationships, modes of rationality, and power (Laurel and Mountford 1990; Long 1999). In their Foucauldian analysis of interfaces, Gupinath Kannabiran and Marianne Graves Petersen (2010: 697) offer a good critique of the conventional reading of the concept of interface in the field of interaction design. They argue that interface is not just a means to achieve desired interaction; it is the very frame in which the contestation and performance of power relations happen. In this view, mundane interactions would be seen as active negotiations of power rather than another step in task sequence.

Thus, the interactions produced by passports should be also understood through a recognition of interfaces as specifically designed and material-historical forms of interactivity that emerge from and shape certain practices and power relations. For instance, the graphic and material reality of the artifact of the passport is an interface. It is designed historically to interact and communicate transnationally with border guards, police, citizens, and its holder. It is designed to call for certain reading and writing practices performed by border guards, travelers, police officers, co-travelers, citizens at airports, checkpoints, train stations, and even in the everyday life of a city (Keshavarz, 2018), and so on. Moreover, it is designed to "excommunicate" (Thacker 2013) forgers, imposters, and border transgressors. But their interfaces are more than the graphic reality or the architecture of information. Passports are not only an example of information design in the shape of an interface between the databank and the body carrying it. They are interfaces that generate interactions beyond a simple product facilitating the flow of information. Like any "good interface design," as illustrated in the widely cited graphic work by Jesse James Garret (2000), passports follow the principles of good user interface and thus hide certain space, materials, technologies, and data, and intensify and expand other aspects of an operating system or technology in the name of user-friendliness.

All of these practices of simultaneous hiding and exposition occur in an ambiguous environment in which certain interactions are invisible to the travelers, who may tangibly experience only one or a few interactions in the moment of border crossing. One example of such ambiguity within the field of interaction is evident in the processes of examination of bodies and their relation to the passport and registered data at airports: what Peter Adey (2009) calls confession. What gives shape to this confession is a set of interfaces and their interactions with each other such as: passports, databases, application forms, agents, kiosks, the legal and thus the physical distance between the body of the border crosser and the representative of the sovereign body, and the monitoring of border crossers' behaviors, facial expressions or bodily gestures by border agents who are professionally trained to detect abnormal psychological reactions in the moment of examination. Contrary to what they are experienced as—a flat space and a linear sense of time, without local history or identity, where everyone is drawn into a senseless and meaningless flow of spacetime (Thackara 2005)—or, as they have been repeatedly referred to, "non-places" (Augé 1995), airports as amplified designed sites of examination and confession in modern time indeed have a strong sense of a particular identity, culture, and politics (Salter 2008; Hall 2015). Contrary to other citizens, in the case of travelers without the "right" papers, airports and transit halls become places for a long stay (Mehran and Donkin 2004; Khosravi 2010). No wonder many grey zones in airports exist today, in which arriving persons without the right papers are interrogated or detained. The place that seems to be a passing step for everyone else has, for some groups, become the final destination, where one destroys her or his passport (real or forged) in order to limit the possibilities for recognizing the country from which she or he has departed or traveled. For travelers without the right papers, the airport is experienced differently. It is a place, rather than a non-place. It has a particular meaning and identity with specific performances to be carried out. With constant changes and updates in security plans and rituals, passports and visa validities, travelers from "certain" countries, who carry less valid and more "risky" passports, experience such places with fear and trepidation. They can never be sure if they have all necessary documents in order, or whether they have complied with all the procedures before their departure. It is in such contexts that designers intervene to make the experience of checkpoints, which are presented as "an interruption in the way of boarding a flight" (Hawley 2007), more interactive for travelers. These interactivities could include different design measures and qualities such as the reduction of the time spent at checkpoints, speeding up the process of boarding as well as deliver enjoyable experiences while waiting in a way that the "interruption" would not be felt. Here, qualities should be designed that are measurable, scalable, and quantifiable (Lisle 2003; Adey 2008; Salter 2008) because they have to be translated into a profit-oriented regime in a global scale. Profit for whom is the question upon which designers often forget to reflect. In order to create a tangible experience of flow and an intangible security plan, certain interfaces need to be designed in a way that will automatically filter out those who are not entitled to the pleasurable experience of uninhibited flow. Moreover, the low-risk travelers are encouraged to participate in the production of promised security through interactive means (Andrejevic 2006). Consequently such designed interactions lead to insecurities of being caught and detained for travelers without the right papers. There has been a shift from strong, explicit, and spectacular monitoring toward less visible methods for low-risk travelers.

It seems not to be enough that travelers are able to travel safely; they have to enjoy their presence at airports. Foucault argues that biopower is concerned with much more than just the lives and the "living" of the population, but rather that people should be "doing a bit better than just living" (Foucault 2007: 327). While the invisibility of monitoring should be experienced as pleasurable for low-risk travelers, monitoring should be intensely felt by high-risk travelers. This is the result of understanding interfaces as isolated and neutral, waiting to be designed in order to deliver specific tasks and actions. This is the result of seeing interaction as something created out of nothing and in an empty place and time. Interfaces promise security for some in a specific site through producing insecurity for others.

Manipulations

As I have shown so far, passports indeed persuade us that they are user-friendly versions of the complex interactions performed by various technologies. We— passport bearers and those who have the task of checking passports' validity and authenticity—do not access "data" through the interface and artifact of passports. In truth, we access a passport that is articulated in a way through which imagined users are able to perform their anticipated behaviors, tasks, and actions accordingly. Since passports are not merely a means to enact those tasks and performances but also an active agent of articulation, the passport is very much part of the interactions it promises to bring. This means that it is important to think of passports not only as interfaces of data and tasks, but also as interfaces that simultaneously generate regimes of practices, inaction, and actions that are sometimes anticipated and sometimes contingent. As Daniel Cardoso Llach (2015: 53) writes in his account of the material history of computational design, "technological systems index their makers' theories of action, thus modeling users, machines, and their interactions."

In a conventional understanding of design, what we—as users—experience by having a passport is a product made out of materials, information, forms, and scales, which serve specific purposes. However, the material and graphic reality in the hands of users is in practice a set of interfaces that associate bodies to data and software, as well as actors who help to engender acts of association. These actors include passport bearers, border guards, police officers, bureaucratic networks, passport-reading machines, airports, and so on. Thus, passports are not a mere product designed by a designer or designers, and then targeted toward users who in this case are assumed to be passport bearers. They are a set of complex interfaces that articulate a series of actions as fluid, fast, and dynamic (interactions) and a series of other actions as cautious, measured, and interruptive (inactions) between various bodies, both human and non-human. Since interfaces mediate actions, interactions, and inactions simultaneously, passports as interfaces target bodies and sites beyond those intended by their initial design. This is why focusing on designing the very graphic reality of a passport is reductive and irresponsible when in practice design is engaged in shaping a complex environment that extends beyond the color of the passport covers or the graphics in its pages. This demonstrates that interactions are not simply objects or things, nor are they a "between" space; rather, they are "mediating environments" (Drucker 2011). These mediating environments transform and expand practices such as reading and writing beyond that specific presumed context of mobility.

This affirms that design does not *create* interactions.[12] If design does anything, it intervenes in interactions that are already in place; it manipulates them and produces other forms of interaction that can partially affirm the status quo or are willing to change it. Design is already part of the environment that it is produced from and the environment that it produces. In this sense, design is embodied in history. Since history is already about interactions in the form of power relations between actors and the capacities of their materialities and performativities that allow them to interact, design is not an external axis able to conduct these interactions from the outside. In fact, design is in an internal relation. It is an actor itself. Designing interactions is thus an act of manipulation and not one of creation.

Paul Dourish (2001), by drawing on his own interpretation of phenomenology, argues that artifacts not only represent the world of their target groups (e.g., users, subjects), but also participate in that world and in activities embodied in it. They are embodied artifacts and thus participate in embodied forms of interaction. To put it simply, artifacts participate in the world they represent. Thus, meaning is not a fixed notion prescribed to artifacts but is rather articulated and negotiated in the interaction of artifacts, humans, and their shared environments. Despite how political this argument may sound, the consequences within design have been surprisingly apolitical. This is why the concept of manipulation—despite its negative associations—captures the destructive and violent aspect of designing that historically and discursively has been pushed aside. To turn away from the innocent presentation of interaction as merely a dynamic relationship between people and things and to locate designing as a form of manipulation is to understand what design activities do when they are a part of shaping one interaction and not another. For instance, while much of design scholarship focuses on how to design a more interactive experience between bodies and artificial interfaces, less attention has been paid to the levels of interpassivity produced by the very same interactions. Designing interfaces for interaction should also be read as the practice of shaping interpassivity. It can therefore be understood as a practice that is inherent to what Gilles Deleuze (1992) calls "control society." He argues that we have moved away from Foucault's disciplinary society (1977) to a society where the aim is no longer to "mould individuals," but rather to "modulate dividuals" (Deleuze 1992: 4). While "moulding individuals" requires rigid enclosures, the "modulating of dividuals" happens through a fluid and dynamic field. Molding tends to fix and demarcate things, but modulation does this through a level of transformation, a possibility of constant change in the frame and format that makes interactions possible, rendering it less visible and invasive but more effective and present. Modulation is not intended to produce an individual, which would be equivalent to the making of a fixed recording. Instead, the format itself is opened to variation in real time (Bogard 2009: 22). Passports are good examples of this. They are not mere artifacts for fixing individuals, and if they were, their designs would have been different. The fact that passports can be extended by having more pages added to them during their period of use, that they can be stamped with entry and exit signs, and with visa imprints or categorical signs at any time, affirms that these artifacts provide the authorities with the capacity to leave traces on them over time, to rewrite them, to manipulate and shape them and consequently to transform the legal, political, and social status of their bearers. Rather than being fixed objects, passports are interfaces, processes, and performances of transformation. Such processes require certain interactivities but also cannot escape the production of interpassivities.

*

Design is always in the field of interactions and tries to make sense of that field through its capacity for manipulation. This is yet again another affirmation of the idea that power is not necessary expressed in the form of mastery or domination but is played out in the field of interactions, "contemplated in a relationship which cannot be disassociated from forms of knowledge. One always has to think about [power] in such a way as to see how it is associated with a domain of possibility and consequently, of reversibility, of possible reversal" (Foucault 2007: 66). There are three points that can be extracted here: first, power is not about dominion but interactions, which means that interactions are not about a set of equal and dynamic forces distributed evenly among interfaces and across bodies. To put it another way, one cannot merely talk about interactions and the way that they might be designed through interfaces without talking about the power relations that their design produces. Thus, interactions are not innocent, neutral, or self-evident. Second, the processes of interactions do not occur in a vacuum, but always already intervene in other interactions that exist in the world. Third, the domain of interactions is a domain of possibilities and the possibility of reversal. While interactions can forge new relations and actions, at the same time, they can easily comply with discourses that promote the inactivity of certain bodies and the deprivation of agency for some subjects. Notwithstanding, seeing power as a field of interaction affirms the existence of a space and time that can open up contingently due to its encounter with things, events, and humans. The task may reside in identifying those moments and localities in order to rearticulate them.

Figure 1 Passport for the stateless, Ahmad Hammoud and Malak Ghazaly, 2016.
Photo courtesy of Mohamed Elshahed.

Figure 2 State of Palestine stamp, Khaled Jarrar, 2013. Photo courtesy of Khaled Jarrar.

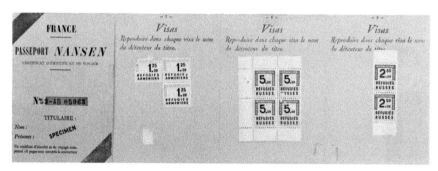

Figure 3 A Nansen passport designed and proposed by Fridtjof Nansen as an international substitute for a passport, which allowed refugees who had lost and/or had been deprived of their citizenship to enter and transit other countries issued by the Nansen International Office for Refugees, 1930–1940. The document shown here is a Nansen certificate with Nansen stamps as visas, used to enable a refugee from Russia or Armenia to travel. Image courtesy of United Nations Archives at Geneva.

Figure 4 Passport of an Austrian Jewish citizen Chane Püder, re-validated with a red J sign issued on October 19, 1938. Visa imprints to Belgium and the UK are visible on pages 8 and 9. Image courtesy of Los Angeles Museum of Holocaust.

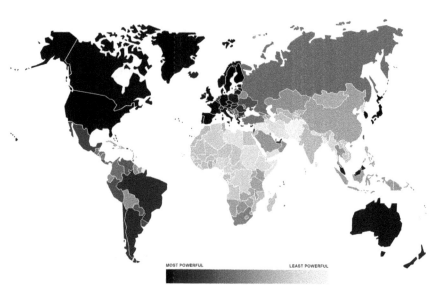

Figure 5 Passport index visualizing the power of passports in giving the ability to move freely, December 2017. Data extracted from Henley & Partners Visa Restriction Index (https://www.henleypassportindex.com) and Arton Capital Passport index (https://www.passportindex.org). Map: remade by the author.

4

Passporting

Histories of the passport and its emergence as a specific device enmeshed with bodies, relations, and interactions through specific local technologies that produce global rationality suggest that their design goes beyond the actual artifact and interface. Thus, passports and their associated practices should be renamed. I suggest the term *passporting*. This is because artifacts are not isolated from the environments in which they function and the environments that they produce, and due to the fact that passports are in constant change and are contingent articulations of power. Furthermore, they are always already in interaction with bodies—biological and artificial. For all of these reasons, they should be renamed according to recognition of their actions and what flows from them. Passporting therefore refers to the practices, performances, and interactions to which the artifacts and interfaces of passports are central. Passports are therefore mediators in passporting politics. The reading, analyzing, critiquing, intervening, or subverting of the politics of passporting, then, requires an understanding of passports as artifices, as materially made articulations that produce sensibilities. The production of affects through *materialities* and *sensibilities* is mediated by two particular practices: *translating* and *part-taking*.

In this chapter, I will develop the concept of design politics further, based on these four modes that provide possibility to think and read the ways in which passporting operates. It will also serve to offer a critical-analytical framework for discussing the concept of design politics and its articulations more broadly. At the same time, these modes of passporting politics offer possibilities of intervention, which is to say, a rearticulation of the mobility regime. I argue that one of these rearticulations is the practice of forgery. I will discuss how each mode of passporting articulates its current regime as well as how each can be used to rearticulate the same regime through forged passports. Thus, while this section is a theorization of how the passporting regime in particular and the design politics of the passport in general operate, it is also about how forgery uses, enables, and rearticulates specific ontological qualities of this regime in other directions than the ones imagined by their initial design. While it is an investigation of politics through the *materialities, sensibilities, part-taking*, and *translating* that the passporting regime generates, it is also about the possibilities of politics through the rearticulation of these four modes carried out through forgery.[1]

Materialities

I: How Thick Is Your Passport?

On popular video-sharing websites, videos in which the narrator presents her or his passport as the protagonist of the film can be found. The goal of many of these videos is to show which stamps and visas the passport holder has been able to obtain or "collect" over a short period of time traveling, often backpacking. In one particular video on YouTube entitled "Pride of the passport," which is narrated by an American woman, she shows her passport page by page and states that she is proud of it as she has collected so many "rare" visas and stamps, to the extent that she is afraid to renew it. She wants her passport to be alive and in circulation. She also mentions the "thickness" of her passport (Figure 7). The thickness is evidence of her freedom of movement. More visas mean more papers have been added to the passport, which makes it thicker, richer, and more valuable. In one of the comments posted on the video we can read:

> You have good travel history, lady. Actually what I noticed is that page with personal information is very very thin. I am a Kazakhstani national, and personal information page in our passports is the same thin as in an American one. I'm not really satisfied with the quality, because I think quality of travel documents could be much higher for money we pay for it. I really like Irish passport for that very hard laminate film they use to protect it (https://www.youtube.com/watch?v=I1bqfzGl3aE).

The materiality of passports therefore offers value, in both a symbolic and a pragmatic way. Everyone who has tried to obtain a passport illicitly knows that a passport with more stamps in it is more expensive. This is because the thickness, weight, and the traces left by many governments upon such passports assert that it has been tested enough. It has traveled enough. It is an experienced passport. In contrast, the thinness of the pages or the thinness of a passport suggests less value, less authenticity, and less respect. This was frequently discussed by many of the border transgressors I met.

Timothy Mitchell argues that the nation-state is manufactured as "an almost transcendental entity, as a nonmaterial totality that seems to exist apart from the material world of society" (2006: 181). Passports can unhinge the so-called non-materiality of the state and point to relations manufactured by states and through individuals. Passports, therefore, because of their materialities— which is a condition of them being devices—orientate bodies and shape space and time in one particular direction and can disorient the same bodies toward other directions.

When passporting practices are materialized in the form of a passport, this material can transfer the border onto the bearers themselves. The border is not actually "there," outside, but "here" and omnipresent, encrypted onto the body of the passport bearer. When the right to move is summarized and materialized in the practices of passporting, the lack of such material presence results in the lack of exactly that right which has been manufactured through the passport: "one assumes that what one calls, in a word, a 'sans-papiers,' is lacking something. He is 'without.' She is 'without.' What is he or she lacking, exactly? Lacking would be what the alleged 'paper' represents. The right, the right to a right" (Derrida 2002: 135).

What gives the narrator of the film the ability to narrate her passport in this particular way? Perhaps it is the form and materiality of her passport, as it is the materiality of the event of border crossing in the form of a book that matters. It is a form of thing-power that speaks for itself without a direct relation to the concept. The pocketbook-sized thing that can be rewritten and reread over time through material practices enables her to construct that particular narrative. But the narrative such materiality allows us to construct, in many cases, is only an affirmative and homogeneous one: that there is, and should be, a "rational" material link between the body, the citizen, and the nation-state. Even though the thickness of the American citizen's passport allowed her to remember her individual experiences of border crossings and her trips—often presented as "exotic" and "funny"—the narrative is still dominated by the fact that having an American passport in hand, as a low-risk traveler, matches the current regimes of identification and representation. An American is free to make her passport thick. Passports are books with one dominant narrative. Creating other narratives however, is not impossible and has been done through many artistic and literary works around passports.

The form and design of passports offer resistance to, for instance, the narrative of the way they are made, produced, constructed, and articulated (Burt 2013). As a book and an e-book, passports' actual production, like their circulation, is also subject to transformation. First, they are generic material; the cover and digital parts are cheaply produced. Then they become national books, American, Swedish, Iranian, and so on through the coat of arms, the graphic designs of the papers, and the information embedded and locked into the chipsets. Finally, they become personalized by the attachment of photos, biometric data, signatures, and so on. The process of the production of such an artifact from a "transnational" commodity to a highly nationalized and personalized device reveals the artifactuality of nationality and citizenship. It affirms that citizenship is a process of material articulation, both in terms of protecting individuals through a book, and in terms of giving access to nationalized material infrastructures. It affirms that it is the materiality of government practices that can shape politics. If the right to move can exist in the form of a book, be made and unmade, and be transformed over time, then we can identify the materiality of any right and any political subjectivity in which design politics is involved. As Jacques Derrida (2005: 61) puts it: "the history of politics is a history of paper, if not a paper history."

II: If One Can Make a Passport, One Can Remake It Too

Certain passports have the potential to become thicker and thus more valuable. However, the histories of passports have demonstrated that this possibility of adding visas, stamps, pages, and new information both digitally and visually can produce different political bodies and subjectivities. The example of the Nazi regime in Germany stamping German Jewish citizens' passports with the red "J" sign is an important one. The stamping of pages transforms the blank passport into a book, an archive with stories of crossing, of being validated or invalidated by various states. In these stories, it is the paper and the materiality of passports that can be reappropriated or essentially redesigned over and over again in order to change or sustain one's individual legal or political status in the global passporting regime. Governments therefore redesign passports through the acts of stamping, visa imprinting, placement of special signs, and addition of temporary clauses to these books. This can be thought as "iterability," a "logic that ties repetition to alterity" (Derrida 1988: 7). Passports as inscribed devices that can be written and read are iterable. However their very condition of iterability makes them subject to alteration by not only the so called official authorities but also forgers who by applying their technical skills iterate the passport in a different context. Forgery is an act of material reappropriation. However, it is not a legitimate redesigning in comparison to what states, as authorized actors, carry out. Forgers are thus able to disrupt the monopoly on the articulations of power that states attempt to uphold. For instance, making a fake passport out of a blank passport by adding information to an authentic blank passport is about giving it a history and bringing it to life. Much like the ways states make certain passports livelier than others, a lively forged passport passes smoothly. This history, however, is not just any history but a particular history engraved into the blank booklet. As much as migrants often fall into ahistoricity in the way they are only geographical, not historical subjects, the device that potentially provides access for them has to take on the task of historicization. A forged passport in one way creates a trustworthy history for the traveler: a history of authorized and regularized movement. The forged passport articulates a material history appropriated for the recognition of the right to move.

Amir Heidari, perhaps the most well-known migration broker in the Middle East and Europe during 1980s and 1990s, with whom I had a lengthy conversation in summer 2015, told me that in 2001, Sweden introduced brand-new passports, which were more secure and harder to forge.[2] A journalist asked him to comment on the security of the new passports:

The journalist wanted to know my opinion about the newly designed passport. I asked him in return, who has made these newly secured passports? "Authorities" he replied. I told him in return, who are the authorities? Human beings, right? Then humans can forge them too. These concepts are abstract. Once citizenship and nationality are materialized with things such as passports then they can become rematerialized ... An Iranian becomes an Italian, an Iraqi becomes a Turk, an Afghan becomes Japanese and so on.

Helene Andersson, the head of the Document Analysis Group at the Swedish National Forensic Center who is tasked with both checking the quality and security of Swedish passports and analyzing the forged passports, affirms Amir's take on the artificiality of the passport: "if one can make a passport, one can forge it too. It is a matter of how much money and contacts to which one has access" (Holmbäck and Keshavarz 2016: 13) (Figures 8 and 9).

Forged passports therefore create a rupture in the order of things and their constructed history through the material interventions they exercise. In reality, it is the very materiality of the world that allows passport forgers to perform such ruptures.

Donald Schön's (1983: 73) famous formulation on design and materiality, which defines "design as conversation with the materials of situation," is also evident in how a forger stays within certain situations and their materialities. However, it is important to remember that the use of the term "conversation" has to be framed, contextualized, and politicized by asking: what kind of "conversation" and among whom? In this book, I use the term "articulations" instead of "conversations." The political possibility that an articulation of materials in a situation offers, therefore, relies on recognizing the existing relations and linkages made and sustained by hegemonic politics—which is to say, a single and dominant narrative offered by the monopolized regime of mobility. This dominant narrative needs to be considered while engaging with the situation—the existence of borders, security guards, passport checks, and the urgency to cross these borders—through rearticulating the materiality of the situation and therefore redistributing the sensibility of it. In this way, forged passports participate in a specific politics of mobility while refusing that of hegemonic politics, which fixes a body in its made nationality, race, gender, class, and its restricted space and time of movement.

Sensibilities

I: I Have Not Seen Such a Passport Before!

As was discussed earlier, the materialities of passports define and transform passport bearers over time. Fabricated and artifactual relations and interactions of power, made tangible through materials and prompted by their specific design, define and distinguish the various "regimes of senses" (Rancière 2006) within which one should be recognized, and being thus recognized, one must play the role or identity that has been assigned. This can be called the "sensibilities" of passports. Thus, by having such material-sensible associations in hand, there are some visible and invisible, sayable and unsayable, audible and, consequently, inaudible subjects and bodies. Passports, therefore, distribute senses according to the materiality they impose, offer, or manipulate. Distribution of senses, for instance, can be seen in how those with better and more valuable passports spend less time in checkpoint lines compared to those with less valuable and less recognized passports. It occurs frequently at airports, when one looks at the passports in the hands of other travelers and recognizes them with an established sensual regime that has previously been ingrained.

In February 2014, on my way to New York via Reykjavik Airport in Iceland, I was selected "randomly" for a special security search. I was guided to a room in the corner, which was not noticeable at all to those who were passing quickly without being taken aside. After the procedure finished, one of the officers looked at my passport. "Hmm, I have never seen this before!" he said. "What?" I asked the officer. "Iranian passport! It is good to see what it looks like!" He replied, and smiled while returning it to me.

The regime of passporting, of course, creates certain visibilities and invisibilities. It does this through already-established constraints, affordances, and validities. Some passports get to travel more than others. Consequently, some are seen more than others. Some passports are more visible, while some others are, conversely, invisible. Nonetheless, there are invisible ones that come under a certain light in a certain time and space, recall their dominant and homogenous narrative, and betray the bearer's individual narrative. The officer in the airport did not open my passport at all, but there was something strange in his hand, which made him react in that way. Suddenly, a new item was introduced to his regime of sensibilities of passports.

Passports, therefore, can be devices for the manipulation of time and space of a traveler by establishing regimes of senses and meaning-making in relation with others as well as governments. On one hand, seen and recognized passports often resemble seen and recognized bodies, whereas on the other, an unseen and unusual passport often warns that an unusual body is around. In the core of passporting, a regime of sensibility emerges in which passports can deliver certain experiences but can also prevent certain bodies from experiencing time and space in the way they wish. Thus, passporting distributes a regime of the sensible. Rancière calls this distribution and redistribution of time, space, and, consequently, experience and collectiveness: a configuration of the visible and invisible, the audible and inaudible, and the sayable and unsayable, the "distribution of the sensible" (2006).

In the logic of the distribution of the sensible, distributing the communal space and time of society, and participation and contribution to spacetime, take place through the perceptible. Therefore, through a predefined and pre-ridged realm, the sensible can perceive and experience something defined and cannot perceive or experience the non-defined (13–14):

> The distribution of the sensible reveals who can have a share in what is common to the community based on what they do and on the time and space in which this activity is performed […] it defines what is visible or not in a common space, endowed with a common language, etc.

In everyday life, this realm of sensibility is predefined, pre-established, or, to put it better, already articulated. Within this realm, some sensory possibilities can be perceived and others cannot. Sensible orders reproduce and enforce divisions within a society: who is qualified to see, listen, or discuss, and who is not; who can exercise the authority over seeing, listening, or speaking. For Rancière, this is not a matter of good taste, but about sensibility, through which some parts of society come together while others are excluded or ignored, which is to say, there is an established "community of sense," through which some are not recognized, resulting in their invisibility.

II: Today, You Are Going to Be a South Korean!

A forged passport, however, redistributes established regimes of senses in its own particular way. Nemat, whose story opened the first pages of this book, was an unaccompanied minor when boarding an airplane bound for Oslo from Athens with a South Korean lookalike passport. When we met in 2012 in Malmö for the first time, he was undocumented. While he managed to arrive to Oslo, his asylum application was rejected because the Norwegian authorities did not believe that he was a minor. Now in Sweden he was planning to apply for asylum again. Despite him not being entitled to move freely from Greece to Norway—he would only have been able to move legally by having a Schengen visa in his Afghan passport—he momentarily exercised his freedom of movement with the service of a forged passport, albeit with lots of fear and anxiety. Viewing this from a global perspective and out of context, an Afghan citizen traveled all the way from Ghazni to Oslo without fulfilling any of the expectations held by international and nation-states' regulations on the way. In this sense, he disrupted the regime of senses that tried to keep him in his place of birth and make him play the role assigned to him by the current politics of mobility. He managed such a disruption because of several refusals he made in the regime of senses.

His ability to walk for several days and nights through mountains and deserts, his social networks in learning strategies of traveling and living clandestinely, and the materially reappropriated artifacts he used enabled him to achieve his goal to some degree. The latter part that enabled him to perform such refusals is what designers are skilled at and can carry out in order to practice politics in a specific direction.

Designers take part in forming a regime of sense, or sensory perception, which takes place in specific spacetime. There are, however, many ways that designers may approach the sensible order. As in the case of the current hegemonic mobility regime, design is complicit with an established sensible order, which engages in the processes of distributing spacetime and affirms or enforces the organization of society in terms of existing groups of those included and recognized. This is the case, as elaborated earlier, with how designers engage in the passporting regime. In contrast, a disruptive sensibility can intervene within the existing or established sensible order, in which those involved actively redistribute the sensible order, thereby also intervening in the social and political order. In this way, an interruption or intervention into the realm of materiality can constitute a redistribution of sensible; a new aesthetical regime of politics, as was discussed earlier in the arguments put forward by Rancière.

The forged passport is one device that in its devising offers the possibility of enacting parts that are not supposed to be enacted by people who are to carry those passports in their pockets. The modification of spaces and time to be opened to other bodies are often registered as a "willful imposition on those spaces" (Ahmed 2014: 147). That is why, in subverting the sensible regime of movement, the image of migrants with forged passports so readily goes hand in hand with that of criminals and terrorists. These images are powerfully circulated in the media and in public discourses because the legalized inhabitants of the spaces restricted to illegalized bodies would like to see such subversions as an invasion of their space rather than seeing it as a political act of opening up alternative possibilities of moving.

Part-taking

I: I Am a Citizen Now!

The sensibilities of the passports articulated through their materialities take us to another layer of the complexity of passporting. This layer is part-taking, in which passports dictate who is part of an established and defined territory (e.g., the European Union) and therefore, who is sharing a part, taking that part and therefore acting or enacting her or his own part. Passports participate in the same world their bearers inhabit. They also participate in a regime of senses, in the predefined and already-articulated realm of visibility and invisibility. They take part in the reproduction of unequal distribution of material infrastructures and rights. They share their thing-power in a control society, and enact violence by stopping bodies in situations where the body, the name, and the passports visibly mismatch one another. In this sense, passports are strong participants of the world we have made and continue to make. At the same time, they offer the possibility of participation in, for instance, the labor market (Anderson 2006). They participate in the regime of citizen-making, which consequently makes individuals legal participants of that regime (Caplan and Torpey 2001; Breckenridge and Szreter 2012). Passports are documents of an imagined community such as nation that is often presented as a "sacred whole" (Anderson 2006). Citizens take part in this whole by carrying passports—

which themselves are part of the whole—while moving outside the whole. In response, paper and material objects such as passports carry bodies that represent the whole, and thus the nation. Passports and bodies therefore make both the whole, and parts, meaningful in a mutual relationship from the sovereign's point of view.

Participation as a quality of modern democracies, in which one is able to take part in forming society by having a say through various routines such as voting, or via cultural means such as public art and participatory design, requires further interrogation. Such understandings of participation, which were brought into the practice of design during the 1970s, have long dominated the way participation is interpreted in design (for example, see Bjerknes et al. 1987; Bødker 1996; Gregory 2003). The case of passporting teaches us that participation is not a flat concept that can be achieved through tools, means, and experiments. For instance, passports are strong and pragmatic devices for both facilitating and preventing participation in the world. They are designed and enacted through a classificatory logic, a logic that is at work in any functioning participation, but is often overlooked by the dominant discourse of democracy. Such dominance exists to the extent that participation is often taken for granted as a democratic experience (Keshavarz and Mazé 2013).

The classificatory logic of passporting can be understood as "ways of distinguishing and grouping the holders according to a set of clear rules about the relationship between people, territories" (Caplan 2001: 51) and nations; between parts and wholes. Passports are participatory devices that make things partake in such a way that a desired "order of things" is achieved. Passports as participatory devices, then, distribute parts in an uneven way. Étienne Balibar (2002: 83) argues, for example, that for a "rich person from a rich country," the passport "increasingly signifies not just mere national belonging, protection and a right of citizenship, but a surplus of rights—in particular a world right to circulate unhindered."

Sajjad is a young Afghan man, who has never seen the country to which he technically belongs. He was born and raised in Iran, where he lived partly undocumented for at least eight years. He moved to Europe in 2009 and has lived in Europe first as an asylum seeker, then as an undocumented migrant, and today as a legalized resident—a process that took five years of his life—

during which he did not have legal access to education, work, and had limited access to healthcare. I met him in 2012 when he was still undocumented and waiting to become eligible to reapply for asylum. He told me about the harsh time he had in Iran and how he had been subject to various types of racism, both from the authorities and from people in the street in everyday life, or in the sweatshops in which he worked. After he was granted asylum in Sweden, he planned a trip back to Iran in the hope of finding his sister, with whom he had made no contact for more than seven years. Now, with a refugee passport in hand—which visibly looks like a Swedish passport—he is planning his trip to Tehran, but also to some tourist zones, which are typically unavailable to many Afghan migrants in Iran. The Northern cities of Iran are often called *Shomal* (the North) by Tehrani residents, and are among the most desirable weekend vacation destinations for the Iranian middle classes and, particularly, Tehrani citizens. Undocumented Afghans do not have the same opportunities as Iranians do to enjoy "the North." This is due to their economic conditions, security bans on movement from one city to another, and certain social hostilities. This means that they cannot be tolerated or recognized as tourists in predominantly Iranian social spaces. Afghans have to play their parts in Iranian society only as cheap labor, and are not welcome to share a part in the North as tourists.

"With a Swedish passport in hand, I can go there, book a room in a hotel, and ask for the hospitality I deserve since I am Swedish now," Sajjad told me.

While understanding his joy, I was thinking about how this could be possible in his situation. The receptionist at any hotel might well register him as a Swedish resident and allow him to book a room, which would not have been possible at all for him without a Swedish passport. At the same time, the receptionist, or anyone else in the North's tourist industry, would identify his appearance as "Afghani," a humiliating word used for Afghan migrants in Iran. A passport grants him a part in the global regime of nationalities, but does not guarantee him the same attitude or hospitality that an Iranian would extend toward an ethnic white Swede. The role his body takes in this context contradicts the part he has obtained through the law. Certainly, participation plays a role here, but there are several contradictions between parts and their roles that come into play. He enacts the part he has taken on now—being a Swedish resident—but his appearance brings forward another part. The Iranian subject recognizes Sajjad's first part through a legal context but considers another part of him through a social context.

This suggests that another term for understanding the complexity of participation is required, a term that would allow us to understand participation beyond the flatness of its given democratic nature. Part-taking is what I call the many shared encounters such as the one in Sajjad's story. Part-taking is not flat. It reminds us that a part is, and can be by its condition, separable from the action that links it to part-taking as whole. Like the story of Sajjad and his encounter with the Iranian national subject, part-taking can remind us that there are other forms such as part-sharing and part-acting that are simultaneously involved in shared situations. Parts involved in participation interact with multiple contexts and actors and thus perform heterogeneous interactions. The articulations produced by passporting in this context, then, should be understood through the diversity within acting parts, perceived parts, and performing parts. This challenges the self-evident notion of participation. Sajjad provides an example of a non-white body, whose appearance in the stereotypical regime of translation already fixes him as "Afghani" within an Iranian social context, and who cannot socially perform his other parts, that is, someone with Swedish legal residency. It does not matter that he holds a legal residence permit from a European country in the form of a passport in his hand. He will only be allowed to participate according to the part he has already been assigned. Thus, the passporting regime as one of the articulations of design politics illustrates that in order to develop a better understanding of the complexity involved in the intersection of design and politics, new concepts need to be introduced. This is why I propose the concept of part-taking instead of participation. If there exists one aspect of politics that is explicit in design, it is the matter of participation, in which both the designed thing and the processes of making and usage not only define and distribute senses, roles, identities, and parts that are to be taken, shared, or performed in particular situations, but also partition spaces and times of participation. Consequently, part-taking, along with materialities and sensibilities, is another mode of reading and intervening into passporting: of understanding its articulations and sketching out the possibility of rearticulation.

II: I Have Flushed Down My Passport

Forged passports, by subverting the regimes of the sensible, redistribute the parts that can be taken, enacted, or shared. They offer other capacities of part-taking to the way we are required to participate in the mobility regime, where our bodies are assigned to certain nationalities. A young Afghan man from an underclass position in Iranian society crosses the border as a young middle-class South Korean student. During this process, some given parts refuse to be enacted and instead, other parts that "do not belong to him" are performed.

Nations are often represented as a sacred whole, a transcendental entity or, in secular terms, as a body. In order to feel that one is a *member* of a body, one must remember that one is a *part* of a body as well. Ahmed (2012), in her discussion on "willfulness," states that willfulness refers to the part that through its willing against the will of the whole has forgotten that it is just a part and nothing more. In order for parts to be become parts they need to acquire a duty. This duty can be thought of as a life duty, which is to say, it must be willing to preserve the life and happiness of the whole body. This means that parts should be sympathetic to each other in order to remain a part or member. This in turn demands a form of obedience. Therefore, if a part is not willing to be only a part, a part that follows its duty as a part, then it threatens to break the whole apart. Ahmed makes this clear when she says: "[a] rebellion [always] is a rebellion of a part." The rebellion or the break in the whole—in the body that calls for certain types of participation—therefore is not a mere conflict of interest, but a willful rebellion of a part as it performs its opposition to its duties, roles, identities, and attributions, which could be perceived as a threat to other parts and the will of the whole, to the smoothness and fluidity of participation. Consequently, it is a form of "illegal" action in the spacetime of partaking. It is a refusal to obey, a refusal to be governed.

However, in the passporting regime, for instance, the destruction of the passport, as only one part or participant of the regime, can give new spaces to other parts. The lack of a passport is not always an oppressive axis. It can also be a strategy. Many of the undocumented migrants that I have met told me about the moment they tore apart or disposed of their real or forged passports during their journeys; they burned them or flushed them down the toilet. They did this as a strategy to materially remove their traceable trips in order to avoid deportation to their own countries or to the transit countries (third countries) from which they came.

Before 1991, any Moroccan wishing to travel to Europe could do so with a regular passport. Since the introduction of the European Union's Schengen Agreement, however, this passage has effectively been closed off to all but a chosen few. Unlike the dominant narratives around the tragic deaths of migrants in the Mediterranean Sea in 2015—which has been frequently referred to as Mediterranean crisis—these deaths are not exceptional to an otherwise peaceful order. According to statistics, the first deaths of a similar kind in the Mediterranean was reported in 1991 in Gibraltar, a few months after the Schengen Agreement was completed with a convention toward a common visa policy. Before this convention many North Africans could travel to Spain or Italy without a visa. The EU project redesigned Europe into a continent without internal borders. But this redesigning could not be done without installing and developing a thicker, more extensive, and more technologically complex border apparatus around and outside of Europe managed by Frontex. One regime of participation was replaced by another. In this introduced regime of participation, designed by the Schengen Agreement, the space of participation is partitioned heavily, to such an extent that those Moroccans who have made the journey irregularly are referred to as the "burnt ones" because they burn their passports before embarking. One can see this gesture as a powerful act of refusing to take one assigned part while being willing to take other desired parts. In fact, "the burnt ones have effectively waived their rights as citizens to legal redress" (Downey 2009: 119).

Thinking about taking a part, refusing a part, sharing a part, acting upon a part, and risking a part is the very essence of participation, understood through the concept of part-taking.

Translating

I: Where Does This Passport Come From?

Passporting through its materialities distributes certain regimes of senses that define who takes which part in such relations. This is done through acts of translating the presentation of things to an interpretation of their meanings based on the assumption that is desired, which is set and designed by power relations and articulations. Furthermore, if technical practices carried out by passports such as writing and reading are central to passporting, then translating is at stake every time such practices are exercised in situations between individuals, as well as between individuals and sovereign powers. The concept of translating in the context of passports can be approached from various perspectives. Here, I try to discuss it from the perspective of representation by continuing Sajjad's story. After he came back from his trip, Sajjad recalled his experience of the airport in Tehran:

"Once I approached the passport control, the officer looked at my passport, looked at me and asked in Farsi, 'Where does this passport come from? Is it Chinese?'"

"'No! It is from Pakistan', I replied. The officer became furious and asked me to behave, otherwise he would send me off to another room for interrogation."

He is Hazara, an ethnic minority group from Afghanistan with a similar appearance to East Asians in the narrow system of ethnic translation that many of us use. The officer surely knew that the Swedish authorities had issued his passport, but he did not want to believe that he could be Swedish rather than Chinese. He preferred to read Sajjad according to symbolic ethnic translation rather than the legal translation demanded by his profession.

Similarly, but within the national borders of a territory, in 2013 during one of the biggest police stop-and-search operations to find undocumented migrants in Sweden, *REVA*, many non-white Swedish citizens were asked to show their passports or ID cards in subway stations, streets, and other public spaces. These instances of racial profiling show the racialized aspect of being undocumented: that being without documentation, besides being an economic and legal issue for the authorities, is indeed a fundamentally racialized condition, which produces frameworks for state racism. The police have to reinforce racialization in order to define who is legal and who is not. Consequently, the police tend to check those whose appearances do not match the normative image of legal bodies: that is, white bodies on the move.

It is clear from an account given by Yamina in an interview with Swedish Radio (2013) that the police in Stockholm in asking for her passport took her Swedishness away from her based on her appearance. The police asked her if her passport was real, or if she had bought it in Botkyrka, a suburb where she was born in south of Stockholm inhabited mostly by migrant residents. "No! It is made in Solna [where the Swedish police issue passports], but thank you for your racist comment. Can I get my passport back?" she replied to them.

When borders are enacted legally on those who are inside a territory "illegally" and in spaces that are not seemingly border zones or lands, then those who are actually deemed citizens find themselves turned into quasi-citizens. The Swedish police's questioning of Yamina's passport is illuminating in this sense.

At the same time, Nemat, who departed from Athens for Oslo, told me that while in Greece, because of his skin color, the size of his frame, and his eyes and looks, he was able to obtain a South Korean passport and fly to Oslo without being caught. As a designed device that enables a series of actions to happen—simultaneous writing and reading—passports have to bridge the gap between individuals, their bodies, and their representations on paper. They therefore try to be a good and honest translator while also allowing for the possibility of "good" translations being made by their readers. The recent implementation of biometric technologies, beyond the security and surveillance discourses (Lyon et al. 2012) we can attach to them, can also be thought of in this way. Brand-new passports aim to provide a space for seemingly transparent translation between the subject, the body, the booklet, the database, and the agent of control interchangeably. But there has always been a gap in such a regime, and there will always be a gap between the person, the nationality she or he is bound to, and the materialization of the identity, be on a piece of paper or stored as a digital file. This is why governments are still desperate to stop the so-called "imposters" despite their claims to produce highly secure anti-counterfeiting passports. This gap is where forgery, counterfeiting, or camouflage practices intervene. While they keep the system of translation in place, at the same time they cause an internal error in good translation that is not always discovered by international and national legal readers. The fact that an Afghan body can be granted the right to pass as a South Korean body is an internal error of translation, which yet again affirms the artificial relations between a body and its bound citizenship. With the simple change of body, the passport still operates very well and the border guard who is responsible for the translation also thinks that the elements match in the way that they should: "This person looks Korean!"

Translations that are made possible through passporting are not always affirmative, but can be interrogative. It happens frequently that migrants who have obtained citizenship of a country in which their bodies or the color of their skin is a break in the represented image of that country become question marks in the process of translating. One becomes questionable when one does not fulfill the expectation of an accord between known regimes of representation and interpretation. Khosravi (2010: 98), in his auto-ethnographical work on borders, writes about how he is subjected to more questioning than ethnically Swedish citizens at Swedish borders. He describes borders as not just a physical or administrative frontier but a "colour bar":

> When returning to Sweden, the border requires me to live up to my passport. While others pass through, I am asked some "innocent" questions to prove that I do speak Swedish, that I can identify myself with my passport. Ironically, the same authority that approved my citizenship and issued a passport in my name mistrusts the relationship between my body and my passport.

Passporting as a form of confession (Salter 2006; Adey 2009) establishes examples of good translations, translations that communicate quickly and deliver the desired meaning in the shortest amount of time. In this context, the body comes to testify together with the passport, intentions, gender representations, and social and economic origins: "If we do not confess in a way that echoes with the story that the examiner has told him/herself about us, then we are suspect" (Salter 2006: 183).

Translating happens through a mix of socio-material associations. The US Department of Homeland Security, after September 11 attacks, began a procedure that asked citizens from so-called terrorist-sponsoring countries to fill out extra forms when applying for visas and to write their full names in their native alphabet and all other possible spellings. In the UK, for instance, the British Passport Office faced the "problem" of reading and spelling non-Western names following the immigration and "naturalization" of colonial subjects whose original language was non-European. In response to this problem, the Passport Office used fingerprints to uniquely identify the bearers (Salter 2003: 94).

The traditional understanding of the task of translation in design, replaces the language of origin with raw material and the language of destination with design outcomes, in order to produce meanings. What is required is a new formulation of translation in design, a new formulation based on a more critical-political position exemplified by the design politics of the passport.

Building on the discussed modes of passporting, one can establish that a "good translation" is a kind of agreement or consensus that matches different sensibilities that are confronted with each other. Thus, a good translation implies a form of consensual politics of translation where "the accord made between a sensory regime of presentation of things and a mode of interpretation of their meaning" (Rancière 2010: viii) is in place. One can say that another politics of translation that interrupts or breaks such agreements and matchings can be conducted in order to rearticulate the passporting regime. Forged passports are an example of these rearticulations. Forged passports are particular devices of translation that do not entirely reject that pre-established regime of translation but are rather, through a minor manipulation, able to offer practicalities to escape from it.

II: Who Speaks Hebrew?

A forged passport, or a forged relation to a passport, is a mediating device of translation in the sense of translating a body, a performance, an interaction, and an appearance into a book and to a database. In the event of successful crossing, what occurs is a good translation, but at the same time the shortcomings of the artifact and its artifactual relations are revealed. These shortcomings, however, are only revealed to the traveler and the forger. The readers—the agent, machines, and other passengers in line—accept that this body can simply be South Korean, but the body her-/himself knows that she/he is not supposed to be South Korean. Therefore, while a good translation concerned with delivering established meanings from the origin to a destination is at work, yet another form of free or literal translation is performed that is concerned with the form. The second thus reveals the cracks embedded in historically constructed concepts such as nations, territories, and borders. In this reading, I am inspired by Walter Benjamin's short essay entitled "The task of the translator" (1969). In this essay, Benjamin frames the translator as someone through whom the light of the content (text) crosses, but in crossing through the translator's body and language, it reveals the cracks and shortcomings of her or his language. A forged passport, if it works well, acts as a transparent device through which the agent is able to see and read the body of its bearer as a match with the nationality declared by that device. However, the traveler with a forged passport knows that that passport is not transparent and the cracks within her or his body, the passport, and the system become visible to her or him at the moment of crossing and to others after the event of crossing. Translation is connected not only to the original text but also to the afterlife of the text, Benjamin (1969: 71) argues:

> [J]ust as the manifestations of life are intimately connected with the phenomenon of life without being of importance to it, a translation issues from the original—not so much from its life as from its afterlife.[3]

In the context of forged passports and their relation to translation, the following story is significant:

> The plan was to go by cruise from Patras to Italy. I had obtained an Israeli Passport. When I approached the border guard before boarding the cruise, he looked at my passport for a while and then he became suspicious. "Where are you from?" he asked. "I am an Israeli" I replied. The border guard looked at the lines of passengers waiting to be checked and boarded, then shouted "is there anyone from Israel here?" Another friend of mine who had also obtained an Israeli passport was in the line. He stepped out and replied: "I am from Israel." The guard asked him to come closer and talk to me in Hebrew to see if we understand each other. We started speaking in Farsi for few seconds. The border guard asked him if I knew Hebrew and my friend confirmed it. We both crossed the border.[4]

What is fascinating about this account is the break that was introduced to the mobility regime and its associations with nationalities as legal subjects in that moment, partly due to the border guard's inability to speak Hebrew. The translation that those two forged passports offered affirms the cracks present in notions of being Israeli or Iranian and in the technical devices used to identify these notions, such as passports, border guards, and machines.

Quite different from Latour's approach to translation in relation to actors involved in a network of relations, which takes us into a form of association or transformation, "a relation that does not transport causality but induces two mediators into coexisting" (2007: 108), Benjamin's translator is not necessarily interested in the co-existence of two sides or "traceable associations," but rather the cracks and shortcomings of the two. For Benjamin, multiple sides become visible only through translation as a political practice: a form of enacting a mismatch in the regimes of sense, which might be perceived as a threat to established and recognized territories, parts and wholes.

*

The operation of the passporting regime as well as forgery through materialities, sensibilities, part-taking, and translating affirms two main points: first, any intervention into the passporting regime is not possible unless from the inside and from its own ontological condition. Second, these rearticulations assert that there has been a limit to materializing and designing the practices of movement regulation. But, more importantly, it affirms that there still is, and always will be, a limit to any act of designing, any material articulation of mobility. As Heidari, the migration broker, argued in our lengthy exchange:

> The new biometric passports are also subject to forgery. Time is an important factor here. You cannot keep all passengers in line to check their biometric data, scan their iris pattern and so on. The biometric is made of something, right? A chipset, new technologies, or whatever. They are not truthful; they all are artificial and thus can be reworked. You know it's like a building, you design it and the building shows its fragility, problems and shortcomings over time. That is where we enter. Before the failed passports get to be redesigned we send a few thousand over the border.

I asked him what he thought about smart gates: "it is impossible to run all airports 24 hours a day with these devices ... These devices will malfunction at some point ... there is a limit to them ... They will overheat, run out of memory or RAM ... sometimes they will not function ... forgers then can occupy that moment" he replied.

Forgery in practice forges relations. It brings non-relationships into relationships. It rearticulates existing relations of passports to bodies, machines, border agents, crossing rituals and performances, among others. In so doing, it shows that existing relations are fragile, limited, and temporary. Forgery is about forging new relations that affirm the artifactual relation between body, nationality, citizenship, and sovereignty. If these relations are artifactual, then citizenship can be thought of as artificial and material. To change the way citizenship is distributed today is to think of its artificial and material essence, and to reconfigure and rearticulate this. This is the task partly engendered by a recognition of design politics and its articulations. As I argue that design is both a mode of acting and a series of material articulations, my argument is also then that a passport, while designed by specific politics, simultaneously designs and allows for a certain politics to take place. Following on from this, a forged passport designs a possible politics, derived from specific politics.

In passporting, local practices of interactivity that transform bodies and individuals into interfaces, through materialities and artifactual relations made possible by technologies of power, form an international regime of senses. This pre-established regime of senses attributes and partitions roles, identities, and duties in order to make a functioning participatory flow possible—evident in the current form of political and economic governance over mobility. When participating in such mobility regime, we often forget that not all the parts perform what has been imposed on them according to their gender, class, and/or race, and consequently the spatial or temporal movement across borders and territories that have been assigned to them. They willfully might enact a part that is not reserved for them. This stops the flow. To continue the flow, a system needs to be designed which is skillfully able to render those offending and willful parts invisible, thus making the flow more pleasurable and valuable for the rest. At the same time, this system exposes those willful parts by criminalizing their will and act of moving.

During the course of my research, I met several travelers without the right papers who had manipulated or, in other words, "forged" their bodies in order to make them correspond to the booklet they had obtained. They had also forged certain rituals and performances in order to live up to various established images of travelers. Within the mobility regime, there are some types of bodies, performances, and interactions that are seen more compared to others. Forgery is partly about identifying those seen and frequently mobile types in order to adopt and re-inhabit them. In the case of Nemat, the young Afghan traveler who obtained a South Korean passport, the migration broker told him that young Korean people his age at Athens's Airport would usually be middle-class high school students there on holiday, often traveling in Europe for a short period of time. Nemat had to adhere to this image, or he would not manage to cross. This was the scenario that he had to simulate and perform in the role given to him by the forged passport, using his body, the knowledge of the migration broker, and the embedded stereotyping and racialization that is at work in border guards' practices. He managed to articulate a relationship that did not exist—him being Korean—without speaking a single word of Korean. He dressed in a certain way, and wore certain shoes and gadgets in order to convince border guards that he was the same as many other South Korean travelers.

The state, by defining people through their passports, articulates a specific relationship and interaction to be performed at national and international borders. Any young South Korean crossing an international border performs a South Korean subjectivity but, more than that, performs a South Korean body from a specific class background. Nemat performed his role as a South Korean with the help of his body, a lookalike Korean passport and a specific choice of airport and airline provided by the migration broker. Nemat rearticulated his body within the international regime of mobility. He asserted that, in truth, he was just like many other young men traveling. However, he had to pay for this rearticulation and wait in Athens for several months in order to find a passport in which the bearer's photo looked like him, because his body was not initially legalized and recognized within the mobility regime as South Korean but as Afghan.

If they operate successfully, forged passports function in the moment and for an act of border crossing to which the bearer is not legally entitled. Forged passports grant a right through a forged material relation. This, however, is a momentary right. If forged and fake passports are able to grant this, then they also disarticulate the political and economic control over freedom of movement monopolized by governments. Forged passports essentially pose a simple but important question: if freedom of movement is a right that has become commodified, then why can passports—the material evidence of such rights—not be bought and sold in the imitative form provided by forgers?

In the next chapter, I will shift to examine the practices engaged in by those willful or offending parts, those criminalized individuals and groups who by promoting small material rearticulations reconfigure their own role and power, their own pragmatism, and their own politics beyond the hegemonic mobility regime. I will continue the discussion of forgery by examining what forgery does and how it operates in a broader political context of mobility, beyond just the manipulation of the artifact of a passport, as has been discussed up to now.

Dissent

The history of domination over mobility is also a history of the struggle to overthrow it. In this chapter, I will locate the practices of forgery and migrant smuggling or, as I call it, migration brokery, within the broader context of the current politics of movement. At the core of forgery and migration brokery an act of negotiation occurs, a mode of technically reconfiguring and materially rearticulating the right to move. If, through the material and performative practices in which forgers excel, the right to move can be granted beyond legal establishments such as citizenship, then what has made a particular nation-state or sovereignty legal is threatened. Forgers, perhaps, remind the sovereign power that its power is exercised through material articulations and that it can be reversed by the very same technique. This is partly why forgery is considered a security threat and has been presented as a matter of violence, of violating the law and the public good. Forgers, by shaping and manipulating the performances and interactions of passports and bodies, intervene locally into the artifact of passports and challenge the imagined solidity or transcendental nature of entities such as nations, territories, borders, and citizenships.

In this chapter, I first problematize the selective criminalization of forgery and migrant smuggling when both states and transnational commercial actors are involved in brokering migration and enabling the mobility of certain classes of people as desired "cosmopolite." The fact that millions of people are stateless and, consequently, left without a passport, while others have more than one passport and citizenship, is illustrative of the unequal distribution of wealth, protection, and opportunity globally. Furthermore, based on three conversations I had with three different smugglers and forgers, I intend to show the complexity of smuggling and forgery beyond its criminalization by the state and media. One of these actors is still active, while one claims to have left the business. The third one is "retired" and is someone who, on the basis of his experience and practice, poses difficult questions about the legitimacy of states by arguing that the state and borders are also practices of forgery in and of themselves.

I sketch out an understanding of forgery as a critical practice. I argue that any critical practice that deals with material articulations of the world cannot but be engaged in a form of violence, since it confronts other forms of violence, which are often invisible due to their historical tendency of being institutionalized and normalized. One of the weaknesses of design practice is the lack of various modes of critique—not only as a way of reflecting on what design does, but also as a way of exploring that which design is capable of. If the concept of the design politics can offer ways of understanding and critiquing and thus intervening in situations, thereby proposing alternative modes of acting in the world politically, then passport forgers should be seen as critical makers. They are individuals or groups who, through their involvement in situations around borders and the urgent demand for crossing borders, have obtained both the power of exploitation and facilitation as a result of the ambiguous power relations they create.

One important issue in this chapter is on the use of the terms "smuggling" and "smuggler." I deliberately avoid using the term "smuggler." This is because it is a politically charged term that is used legally and politically without much reflection or care to refer to any illegalized activities arranged across borders. Smuggling includes a wide range of activities from trafficking drugs, food, and humans to trafficking animals. It also refers to practices of contrabanding, often associated with the economic strategies of geographically, socially, and politically marginal communities in borderlands. It is also about migrants who, by paying some amount of money or labor, cross from one country to another. The latter is the specific practice of smuggling that I address in this chapter and, to avoid confusion, I use the term "migration brokery" instead of "smuggling." There are secondary quotations in this chapter that use the term "smuggling." I have not altered these, as I want them to maintain their original appearance.

Criminalization of Migration Brokery

Forgery is an offence, a crime "that cause[s] harm to others," as described by the *Oxford Dictionary of Law* (Martin 2009: 209). The historical practice of forgery has always been a concern for the authorities, owners, and consumers, regardless of whether one is buying an artistic masterpiece, a legal document, or a handbag (Schwartz 1998; Fahrmeir 2001; Groebner 2007; Crăciun 2009). In a commodified world, where things have exchange-value beyond their use-value and obtain this value through the social, economic, and political relations they are able to maintain and reproduce, there will always be copies of the original, of the authentic, and of the valuable. Unlike forgery in art, which is an attempt to make one copy completely identical to the original one, in design, forgery is possible because of the reproducibility that designed products offer. It was said in Chapter 2 that modern passports gain their authenticity not from the original handwriting of the king signing them but from the reproduction techniques monopolized by their makers: governments. Since there is no concept of authenticity or "aura" in the modern notion of passports and sovereign power, and since they comprise material practices, they are thus also vulnerable to other material interventions. If authorities manipulate time, space, and the experience of travelers through passporting, they should know that due to the materialities of these practices, there could be other manipulations too. Forgery is another form of manipulation—a counter-manipulation, even—that produces its own space of power relations and at the same time its own functionality and use-value. Since it operates outside the space of sovereign power, forgery is considered a violent act, often represented as a crime linked to trafficking, terrorism, and other "mafia"-controlled criminality.

Within the policy discussion on migration, a strong consensus has been established that the "smuggler" is the greedy exploiter of the vulnerable migrant. The image that is created of "smugglers" often fits very well into discourses on security and the war on terror. However, as Ilse van Liempt (2007) shows in her empirical study, the reality of smuggling is more complex and she thus calls for a more nuanced approach to the phenomenon. For instance, smuggling can be a way of socializing for migrants who are in transit, or it can be used as a means of making money for their next trip, since migrants usually reside in transit countries irregularly (Papadopoulos et al. 2008; Khosravi 2010; Baird 2014).

Gabriella Sanchez (2014), in her study of migration brokery across the US-Mexico border, argues that non-state-sponsored migration brokery can also be thought of as a set of services provided in order to facilitate clandestine border crossing. Based on her concept of "security from below," she opposes the dominant narrative around illegalized border crossing and migration brokery that simultaneously conveys two strong images. On one hand, this narrative portrays "smugglers" as benefiting at the expense of asylum seekers and migrants through their violent and exploitive practices. On the other, it reductively depicts illegalized migrants as infantile and ignorant individuals who put themselves at risk by blindly following orders. While the highly racialized, hypersexual, and greedy male from the Global South has been the dominant media image of the migration broker, Sanchez shows instead how families play an important role and have agency in negotiating and facilitating what she calls "extra-legal border crossing services" on the US–Mexico border. According to her, illegalized migration brokery can sometimes be understood as a collective-, community-, and solidarity-based process rather than as a set of individual efforts toward mobility.

The criminalization of migration—more specifically border transgressors, illegalized travelers and migrants, and migration brokers—as a central policy (Simon 2007) thus does not let us see smuggling as a set of specific practices that generate knowledge beyond the actual "crime" and for instance reveal the ways in which borders, citizenship, and the state operate in their material and performative levels.

When, in March 2014, an airplane flying from Kuala Lumpur to Beijing disappeared from sight, the very first news concerned an attempt to identify and recognize two bodies that did not match their passports. Two people had crossed the checkpoint with Italian and Austrian passports later discovered to have been stolen in Thailand three years earlier. Both travelers were refugees trying to enter Europe to seek asylum. This was a typical case of blaming travelers without the right papers as the main suspects of any unusual event or, in this case, disaster. Here, the overriding narrative is that one illegalized act—crossing a border with forged passports—can be readily linked to any other illegal act such as airplane hijacking. Furthermore, it seems that the narrative of passports being lost or stolen has dominated the discourse of border security as the only way that passports can fall into the hands of anyone but their legal owners. Passports are not passive objects, and if they are stolen because of their value, their owners can also sell them for the very same reason. Many European backpackers sell their passports in irregular passport markets when they run out of money on long trips and "explorations" in Asian and African countries. They can then announce that their passports have been lost or stolen and easily get an emergency passport through their consuls in order to continue their trips back "home."

On a hot summer day in a city in Central Europe in 2014, Bagou, a young man from West Africa who used to be a migration broker—or, as he puts it, used to help people to get out of Greece—described the "lost passports" situation as follows:

> The price to sell one's passport starts from 300 to 700 euro. There is no robbery as far as I know but there is a selling market for sure mainly provided by young European travellers. However there have been few cases when people left their passports for someone else in order to help that person to cross the border and then reported it as stolen.

When I asked about the phenomenon of "popular passports"—the notion that there are certain countries like Sweden that claim their passports are popular in the market and thus need to be more securitized (Justitiedepartementet 2015)— Bagou denied it:

> It is not about popularity of this or that passport. It is always about what can work or can be guaranteed more than the other. It depends on who is carrying it, at which border you are using it and which destination you are going to. People have to try, try and try again, they fail, but they try again.

Bagou tried to enter Europe several times himself from 2004 to 2010 by various means, and at different points of entry by boat, airplane, truck, and on foot, but never managed to get through until he was granted a residence permit through marriage. It was then that he decided to help other people to get out of their difficult situations in Greece: "Greece is not a destination for asylum seekers, refugees and migrants. It is always a transit spot and this is why I never brought anyone to Greece but smuggled people out from Greece to Central European countries," Bagou said.

When I asked him about migration brokery and how much he has benefited from it, he looked into my eyes and said: "Look, at least for me and many others I know, this was and is a strategy of survival and not a profitable job. We do this for a short period of time until we collect enough money for a safe and secure trip to somewhere where getting asylum will be guaranteed." Bagou's story contradicts the dominant image of smugglers represented in the media and through national and international policies. When you compare the price offered by Bagou, which was confirmed by other brokers and travelers without the right papers, to that of the fee charged by countries that legally sell the right to residence and, ultimately, citizenship, the selective criminalization of migration brokery is exposed.

Different Brokers of the Mobility Regime

In 2014, the Maltese government announced that it would be selling passports to individuals classified as "high value" for €650,000. This is not a new practice. Accessing permanent residency and eventual citizenship through financial investment is a common practice in many countries, particularly in Western or "desirable" ones. Foreign investors who hold £10m of their total money in the UK, for example, can apply for permanent residence after two years of living in the country. In the United States, Immigrant Investor Visas are awarded to foreign nationals who invest $1m in the economy and create ten full-time jobs for US citizens within two years of arrival. Those who do so are awarded permanent residence and, after three more years, can apply for full citizenship. Greece, Cyprus, and Macedonia offer what has become known as "fast-track resident permits" to foreign investors who spend a minimum of €250,000 to €400,000 in the country. EU Passports or US passports are high-value commodities as they are granted to "high-value" foreign nationals. If passports that provide, for certain bodies, fast-track border crossing, freedom of movement, and, more importantly, legal protection in of the form of citizenship are chargeable items—therefore commodities—then why can't copies of them be traded for lower price? Given the neoliberal promotion of competitive markets, why not think of forged passports as commodities that compete with legally issued passports? Forged passports are less functional in their inability to grant citizenship rights, but they are also traded for a lower price. Is this not how the free commodity market works today?

The case of the criminalization of passport forgery and of unauthorized migration brokery affirms the neoliberal logic dominating the exclusive circulation of products and wealth worldwide. Moreover, and as Edward Kleinbard (2011: 702) writes, "Stateless persons wander a hostile globe, looking for asylum; by contrast, stateless income takes a bearing for any of a number of zero or low-tax jurisdictions, where it finds a ready welcome." When it comes to commodities and practices that threaten the hegemonic order of the movement of bodies and, most importantly, cheap labor, then the market is highly regulated, sanctioned, and state-controlled.

Furthermore, there is no clear line between illegalized individual brokers and legalized brokers. In many instances, strong legal actors and authorities engage in seemingly unauthorized acts of facilitating movement across borders. Historically, we know of the stories of diplomats and other powerful actors who, by having access to governmental infrastructures, were able to issue papers for Jews fleeing Nazi occupation and, in doing so, save them from the Holocaust.[1] Technically speaking they were "smugglers," but today they are recognized by various states and institutions as "heroes." In the contemporary world, when moving between territories, states do accept the issuance of false and incorrect passports when engaging in espionage. American diplomats were smuggled out of Iran on false Canadian passports during the hostage crisis in 1979. Canada recently discovered that Israel had been using its passports in order to insert agents into Jordan and Palestine (Salter 2004). A CIA report from 2011 was leaked by WikiLeaks in which undercover agents using forged passports were given specific instructions on how to behave in certain airports and in encounter with border guards if they were selected for secondary screening (WikiLeaks 2014).

In recent years, with the help of business mediators and citizen industry consultants such as Henley & Partners and Arton Capital, Gulf countries have come up with a strategy of turning their stateless populations, termed *Bedoon* (literally means without), into legalized migrants, not by giving them residence permits or citizenship of the country in which they reside but by buying them citizenship from the Comoro Islands. They have bought the passports in exchange for aid funds and development projects. Bedoon, a diverse and heterogeneous group of stateless individuals who have fallen out of the modern registration systems following the independence and formation of Kuwait and the United Arab Emirates, are considered "illegal immigrants" by these states. This move has been criticized by Bedoon activists and bloggers who for a long time have been advocating for citizenship rights in a country where only 10 percent of the population are citizens. The rest are workers and stateless individuals. The initiative allows the Gulf countries to continue their exploitation of labor with greater legality as well as enabling the deportation of these individuals at any moment they desire. Without passports, Kuwaiti or UAE authorities could not deport Bedoon. Both Kuwait and the UAE have silenced dissident voices in order to continue with their project of buying citizenship for Bedoon. As Hakeem al-Fadhli, a Bedoon activist from Kuwait, puts it: "The Kuwaiti government is engaging in apartheid against the Bedoon. [...] We will not allow them to sell us to Comoros. This is human trafficking crime" (Abrahamian 2015: 143).

During the peak of what was frequently referred to as "refugee crisis" in media by journalists, experts, researchers, and politicians, the EU started a long process of negotiation with Turkey in order to return refugees who come irregularly to Europe back to Turkey. In the words of Amir Heidari, this is an explicit human smuggling deal (Holmbäck and Keshavarz 2016). Both states and business sectors are involved in the brokery of migration and irregular mobility, legally and illegally. However, there are certain groups that are cast as the "criminals" and as "the root causes of irregular migration," in the words of EU politicians. One example of this is the Valetta Process, an agreement between EU and African countries to manage "irregular migration" through fighting "criminal networks" and "smugglers." In reality, this agreement, along with the Khartoum and Rabat processes, is nothing but "blackmailing African governments with development aid to accept the European externalization agenda" (Korvensyrjä 2017) through projecting and expanding European borders beyond its territory, making the police forces and governmental infrastructure of these countries a part of European border regime. These have been seen as neocolonial practices where the EU not only uses its position to impose its political and economic will on African countries in exchange for aid and economic development, but enacts the very practices that were internal and constitutive of the European Union project from the beginning (Hansen and Jonsson 2014).

Of particular note is the reuse of *laissez-passer* (European travel document) in the deportation of individuals to their countries of origin—or the ones Europe considers the origin. A document that was originally designed to recognize stateless persons and grant them a temporary right to move has now become used in order to facilitate the deportation of the very same group. On August 23, 2016, French authorities issued a laissez-passer to a supposedly national subject of Mali in order to be able to deport him. However upon arrival in Bamako, this could not proceed further as Malian border guards could not prove the authenticity of the document or the identity of its bearers. The Malian government made a statement to remind all airline companies that they would not accept anyone entering Mali with such a document and that in such cases they would have to return them back to the European country from which they were deported (Allincluded 2017). The EU is now pushing for the general acceptance of this document and is even planning to redesign it from an A4 paper document to one with biometric features (European Commission 2015), giving it more spectacular features and a more "designed" look in order to persuade African countries that it is authentic because it looks like any other contemporary standard passport. Through their selective criminalization of migration brokery and by framing "smuggling" as the main cause of irregular mobility, states successfully manage to shift the focus from their own brokerage deals and violent monopoly over the mobility toward criminalized individuals instead.

Migration Brokers of the World, Unite!

It is simplistic and ethically problematic to consider those who forge passports for others who do not have one or do not have a "good" one as criminals. The story of Amir Heidari, one of the most well-known migration brokers in Sweden, affirms this. I met Amir in June 2015 in a European city where he was living in a camp, had applied for asylum, and had been rejected due to his "criminal" records in Sweden. That summer he was awaiting a decision on the appeal he made against the rejection of his asylum application. Now in his 60s, Amir has been working to deliver migratory services for thirty-five years. He has been arrested several times. In 1995 he had his Swedish permanent residence permit withdrawn and he has served several prison sentences in Sweden and other EU countries, amounting to fourteen years of his life: a two-year sentence for falsifying documents; a four-year sentence for "human smuggling," and a four-year sentence for holding seventy forged passports, to name but a few of the charges he faced in Sweden alone. In 2004, he received a decision that he would be deported to Iran, but because he had obtained refugee status in the 1980s, it was difficult to deport him. Finally, in 2010, Sweden deported him to Iran. He was arrested there, sent to prison, and interrogated. In 2011, he managed to escape Iran once again. Amir, who claims to have helped 200,000 refugees move safely over a period of thirty-five years and to have enabled people to successfully reach different destinations in Europe and North America, with 40,000 reaching Sweden alone, today lives as a stateless person. Born to Kurdish parents in Iran, Amir started his political activities after the 1979 Revolution. He was in his twenties when he joined a guerrilla socialist movement in Iran. After being shot and receiving severe injuries to his legs during armed struggle against the Iranian Revolutionary Guards, he escaped to Turkey and then to Sweden. He became frustrated when he saw how Kurdish people were rejected by every country and were trapped in Turkey, where they faced deportation to Iran and certain persecution. Amir tried to get help from the UN and Western countries to put pressure on the Turkish government in order to cancel the deportation of Kurds to Iran but he received no support: "I realized soon that no one would help us. I started my movement, which has not finished yet. I decided to send people in need of safety" (Heidari cited in Khosravi 2010: 106). Amir argues that he did this as an act of resistance and not for financial gain. In an interview given while in prison, Amir said, "If I moved rice instead of people from one country to another, I would have had huge capital by now and not be here [i.e., in prison]" (Khosravi 2010: 110). Amir told me that he has stopped working as a migration broker but he continues to help and give advice to refugees and asylum seekers on how to apply for asylum in order to be successfully granted a residence permit: "The struggle has taken another form," he told me with a smile on his face. What distinguished Amir from many other migration brokers was that he openly spoke about his activities in the media and public sphere:

I was mostly wanted and hated by Swedish authorities because I was publicly telling about my activities. This annoyed authorities as if they were useless. They looked useless in the eyes of the public. Not only was I making holes and cracks in the system but I was also revealing it to the public and making a spectacle out of it. I had a website, giving lectures, writing debate articles and featuring on TV programs. The main reason they persecuted me was not my violation of the law but violation of the image of the state as the protector of people.

Amir's long-term commitment to the struggles of refugees and asylum seekers cannot be denied. Journalists and academics have written extensively about him and his political ideologies (for instance, see: Heidari et al. 2005; Jonsson 2008; Khosravi 2010; Holmbäck and Keshavarz 2016). He will never stop his struggle, and he believes that this is the reason why the authorities deported him. They knew that as long as he was in the country, he would keep bringing refugees to Sweden no matter how many times he received criminal penalties.

Amir was committed to this cause in a practical form, intervening in material infrastructures, which helped thousands of refugees without the right papers to safely and securely cross borders. During our interview he told me how, during his thirty-five years of experience working to facilitate migration, the state has repeatedly developed new, secure passports that supposedly no one would be able to forge:

> But we and others did forge them. They always promise the most secure anti-counterfeit passport but it never works. Never. When you make it, it might look fully operative without any problem, malfunction or failure, but after a while it shows its problems. Then you have to fix it and redesign it. Before it gets redesigned, we send a few thousand over the border. And this is a story that will continue. It is a story of a rabbit and a turtle as I told once to my persecutor. I told him we are always ahead of you while you think you are ahead of us.[2]

Amir's practices of migration brokery and forgery affirm the possibilities offered by passports for the rearticulation of relations. What Amir did over three decades was to requalify passports for those individuals who have failed to be qualified as citizens: refugees, asylum seekers, and stateless persons. He works for "those who are declined visas and passports. […] for anyone who has no passport" (Khosravi 2010: 109). Amir's knowledge and skills were put into practice to provide protection and the facilitation of freedom of movement.

Amir believes that this is a revolution. If all migration brokers across the world were to organize a unified mass migration for all those stateless persons in camps, all those asylum seekers in transit countries, and all those migrants stopped by borders from the Gulf of Mexico to the United States, from Libya and Turkey to Europe, then this would not look like smuggling but a revolution by revolutionaries not armed with lethal weapons, but merely with their feet, exercising their right to move. These masses pushing the borders of the United States, Europe, and Australia would shake the world and its order articulated by walls, passports, fences, and guards. Refugees "neither rely on nor believe in the world order that has been created. Neither do they recognize where the borders have been drawn" (Heidari et al. 2005). In interpreting these movements as a revolution Amir depicts "a democratic revolt that is taking place outside the framework of our vision of the world" (Jonsson 2008: 175). He depicts a practice of politics that redistributes the sensible, a rearticulation of the politics of movement by those whose part in mobility regime is not determined by their selves.

We Police the Police

Unlike Amir and Bagou, who have stopped working as migration brokers for different reasons—Amir because he was deported from Europe, and Bagou because he stopped of his own accord—Badaud is still active in providing services. Badaud is a young migration broker, who I met first in France in 2013. Over the last four years we have met both face to face and over the Internet several times. Badaud saw the horrible conditions of his fellow travelers in Turkey while in transit and realized that he could both help them and make some much needed money at the same time. I have met with him in various European cities as he is constantly on the move. Throughout the many occasions we have met personally and via the Internet, it was only toward the end of our rounds of conversations that he began to speak of his own history. We spent one and half days together endlessly walking around the different suburbs of Paris as he narrated his experiences of smuggling and being smuggled. By the end of the day, tired of walking, we sat on a bench in the yard of a suburban residential complex as Badaud told his own story of his route from Africa to the Middle East and Europe and how his experiences of being in transit in many countries taught him that: "If you are smart, willing to help and protect your people then it is not hard at all to move people in need of escape." He told me about his first two failed attempts at crossing by boat from Turkey to Greece, and his incarceration in a Turkish prison for about nine months. As he smiled bitterly, he told me:

> When people move as refugees or irregular migrants not all of them die as statistics say, but in truth they get lost in transit, in different prisons and detention centres in various countries where no one can identify them or speak their language. I have witnessed many who their relatives assume are dead, drowned or killed on their way to Europe but in fact they were lost in transit for several years. They are dead in a way but still alive.

Badaud started his business by figuring out how he himself could get out of his transit situation. Later, this became a means of communication, socializing, and visibility while in this situation, which for him lasted three years. Badaud, like any other migration broker, believes that Europe can never fully close its doors because the demand of migrants will always lead to new ones being opened. He consented to talk to me and share some of his knowledge as long as I respected his rule: not to try to know more about his business than him. This meant that he would be the one deciding what to tell me about his business, and if I tried to talk to someone other than him about his work, he would stop talking to me. I accepted the rule. What follows is an excerpt of part of our last long conversation in June 2015.

Mahmoud: How do you find forged passports, I mean how do you get the documents that you need to work with?

Badaud: Mostly online and of course through the networks and trusts that I have established over several years. But you know the main sellers are those who work for the governments, the police. They benefit a lot from our business.

M: How does the forged passport work in the moment of border crossing? I have heard about performances or rituals that you teach to border crossers, is that right?

B: A person who carries forged passport should always know that he is the only one knowing his passport is forged. This gives you confidence in performing according to the passport and what border guards want you to do. You have to behave normally to cross otherwise crossing might become hard. Once one of my clients was going from Athens to Amsterdam and she was asked in the passport control, what colour taxis in Amsterdam have and she could not answer. This is not my problem. I provide the service and basic information and it is your task as a border crosser to prepare fully in terms of knowledge, performance and confidence in order to be able to cross with a forged passport. You should always remember no one knows that you have a fake passport except you. I always tell my clients that the only difference between them and the police is a uniform. It's the uniform that makes that person who is checking their passport into a police officer and nothing else. We mostly work on stereotypes. I mean we play the stereotypes. Most of my clients are black. Many times we might go in group, then one black person who has legal documents—if she or he sees the opportunity—will play that stereotype of carrying drugs or being part of some drug cartel. This often works as European police usually sees black people associated with drug crimes. By disturbing police, other border crossers might cross easier. We police the police. We misdirect the police in one direction and we go another direction where the police are less present. This is not only about passport forgery but border crossing on the sea and land as well. Also we work a lot on different racist practices that exist within European police work. They often fail to distinguish one black person from another. What we do is to abuse that inability or insensitivity which is a form of racism in favour of our people to push them over. This is why lookalike passport and imposter techniques work very well for black people in crossing European borders.

M: "Pushing them?"

B: Yes, helping people to cross. We call it pushing them over the border.

M: Which passports are the most popular ones?

B: My clients often ask for passports issued by French speaking countries because they can pass the language test if it happens at the border. But most of them would like to go to Germany because there is this belief among them that Germany grants asylum easier.

M: What about Scandinavian counties?

B: No! My people do not consider Scandinavian countries as part of Europe.

M: What do you think about the tragedies in Mediterranean Sea?

B: I do not work with boats. I only work with passports and European
      ID Cards. Europe constantly reports on death of migrants and at the
      same time lets migrants die so the rest would be afraid to cross, to
      come. But this never works. Others always say if those who are dead
      could not make it, it does not mean that we cannot make it. When you
      are desperate to move and save your life you never think of what has
      happened to others on the route because you have no other option.

M: How is the business now?

B: Not good. It has become hard recently. Police in Greece have figured
      out our techniques. Also the cost of forgery is rising which the migrants
      have to pay. In addition, people fail a lot in their crossing with forged
      passports and this costs us.

M: How much do you make per month?

B: It depends. Sometimes I can make good sum of money and sometimes I
      have to pay from my own pocket. So it's not stable.

M: How do you get your clients?

B: I do not go after anyone. They contact me. When your service is reliable,
      you do not need to go after clients.

M: What do you think about migration brokers who abuse their clients?

B: I do not know. It is part of the reality of smuggling. Of course it is
      harsh. But famous smugglers never do this. That's why they gain a
      reputation.

M: Do you have any policy in charging your clients? Like charging your
      country mates less compared to others or something similar?

B: No! Not really. But what I do is often a pair making technique.
      Sometimes there are people who have money but no confidence in
      crossing illegally. While you have other types who are very confident but
      poor. I pair these two types together, charge the rich more and charge
      the poor less and tell them that they should go together. I never tell them
      what is the reason behind pairing though.

M: Do you want to continue this business?

B: No. Look, when I left my country I was just thinking to start a business
      in Europe but that needs a lot of money. I do this temporary to finance
      myself. I stopped for two years previously but started again. It's easy to
      get in but hard to get out.

M: So Badaud, I have this residence permit card issued by Sweden. For how
      much would you buy it?

B: I do not care about it that much. I might buy it for 400 euros maximum
        since you are white. But if you were black I would have bought it up to
        1,000 euros.

M: But I am a non-white too. I am from Iran.

B: In my business you are white or at least a fake white. In addition, most of
        my customers are black so your card is not that much of use to me.

I kept in contact with Badaud after this last meeting. At the time of writing this
book in autumn 2017, we still keep in touch via the Internet from time to time.
Once, while wishing me good luck with my writing, he said that he had written
out his story, the reason for his journey, why he became a migration broker,
and what brutalities he had had to face on his journey from his home to the
last EU country he had arrived at in full detail. However, he reminded me that
he would give it to me only once he felt completely safe with me.

The story of Badaud and Bagou is similar to the stories of other migration
brokers and middlemen I met during the course of this research. Often they
are migrants in transit, being exploited due to their clandestine existence and
finding ways to help their fellow travelers while making money. After a while,
they leave the business to start a legal and safe business, but they are all far
from the accepted establishment image of rich smugglers who make enormous
amounts of money from travelers without the right papers.

Forged Passports as Material Dissents

Different in their exchange-value, both regular and forged passports affirm
the materiality of citizenship and freedom of movement. While the expensive,
real, authentic, high-value, and long-term passport is an affirmative material
practice, the less expensive, counterfeit, forged, low-value, and momentary
counterpart is a critical one. However, it is not a critical artifact of negativity.
It criticizes through the affirmation of the ways the passport and mobility
regime works. This can be seen as a sort of "affirmative criticality," to borrow
Clive Dilnot's (2008) term. This affirms that the movement facilitated by
forged passports is a critical material practice because it produces its own
space of functioning by refusing to engage in the legal space that is dominant
and hegemonic. In fact, it affirms that despite states' attempts to totalize and

monopolize the space and time of governance over mobility, there will always be spaces left, or spaces produced that escape from such governance. These spaces are the "space between bodies, law and discipline" (Asad 2004: 279). The contribution of forged passports is to reappropriate such spaces and turn them into other productive spaces of economy, politics, and criticality, however informal or illicit.

The call that forged passports are able to make for subversive intervention turns what is supposed to be untouchable into a threat against its issuing and protecting source. In this sense, the political practice of materiality enacts and releases other forces of material, thing-power, which are suppressed and packaged under certain forms of sensory regimes, designs, and technologies. A forged passport as an internal contract—the inauthenticity of which is visible only to the forger and the user—is a form of material dissent and yet another material declaration of the fictitious—and simultaneously artifactual— relation between the nation and the body. Since they target certain areas, forged passports reveal such absurdities while resisting certain ways of moving or participating in the world. Forged passports can be understood as one of the ways in which the design politics of the mobility regime is rearticulated, not through any universal condition, but through very situated, specific, and local practices and knowledge. Forged passports are thus a material critical practice within the possibilities offered by design politics.

To think of forged passports as forms of material dissent is to think of what the materiality of passports offers for dissenting within the conditions in which the passport is central: (im)mobility. Dissent here is not merely an expression of conflicting ideas or disagreements. Dissent here can be understood as a material mismatch within the artifactual relations produced around the abilities of bodies vis-à-vis their right to move. This mismatch points to moments when a name, a body, or a role in relation to its material manifestation and translation appears at the wrong time, in the wrong place. This mismatch in regimes of identification and representation results in a form of disidentification or "dissensus" in Jacque Rancière's term (1999), which expresses new possibilities of taking part in politics. Therefore, politics in this sense is not only declaring a break from what is assigned to the non-counted parts by the hegemonic mobility regime but also staging and manifesting this non-counted part, as a collective unity. This simultaneous disarticulation and rearticulation is indeed a gap, a dissent within the whole.[3] In this sense refugees, asylum seekers and travelers without the right papers who use forged passports can be thought of as "fluctuating performers" who "bring the nonrelationship into relationship and give place to nonplace" (Rancière 1999: 89).

These dissenting acts performed within the current mobility regime can be seen as specific forms of critique that are different from an act of judgment. The practices of forging passports and using forged passports become clear as acts of refusal in relation to what the global regime of mobility imposes on certain bodies. Forged passports, then, are devices through which the migrant refuses to be fixed, immobilized, and placed in UNHCR lines and camps. Forged passports become one of the ways asylum seekers can enact their refusal and their will to move, in two parts. In the case of "successful" border crossing, the possibility of momentarily enjoying freedom of movement is provided and, practically, the traveler can reach her or his desired destination and apply for asylum. In the case of failure, when the passport or the relation between the bearer and the authentic passport is identified as forged, she or he becomes visible through the defiance she or he has made toward migration policies conducted by national and international actors. The second, however, might cause several losses for the traveler such as detention and deportation, as well as economic punishment.

The critique that forged passports offer, then, is in line with the concept of the "art of not being governed." Critique thus becomes a practice, a counter-art that limits or shows the limitations of the arts of governing, in Foucault's words (1997: 44–45):

> As an act of defiance, as a challenge, as a way of limiting these arts of governing and sizing them up, transforming them, of finding a way to escape from them or, in any case, a way to displace them, with a basic distrust, but also and by the same token, as a line of development of the arts of governing, [...] I would very simply call [them] the art of not being governed or better, the art of not being governed like that and at that cost.

This does not mean that one should learn or understand how not to be governed at all, or become ungovernable per se, but, rather, "how not to be governed like that, by that, in the name of those principles, with such and such an objective in mind and by means of such procedures, not like that, not for that, not by them" (44). Therefore, the art of not being governed is often a momentary refusal—in the moment of identification, of crossing a border—in relation to a set of principles—passporting—which show the limits of governance at a particular cost—the possibility of detention and deportation.

Critical Designers of the Mobility Regime

Forgery—beyond being a specific way of practicing critique as material dissent and as a situated act of refusal—is also different from the common practice of critique that starts from the legitimate foundation of power by questioning its discourses. Forgery starts from how power operates in its design, details, procedure, technical measures, its malfunction and breakdowns—and by doing so it brings down the mystic, grand claims of power to the reality of an operability via materials and within the material world. Here "because the critic is a technician, she knows that every system is plagued by its frictions or its bugs. Because she has learned to observe the official documents with the eyes of a forger, she knows that one should never take at their word the great discourses that power promulgates about itself" (Chamayou 2013). This technical mode of critique both performs within and imposes the materialities of the authority over the right to move. In this sense while it is an affirmative act of critique, it nonetheless exposes the vulnerability of the state and its borders, revealing to us the very mundane materials that constitute such seemingly solid, unchangeable, and hard entities (Figure 10).

The critique practiced by those using forged passports is not a privilege, a distant position that echoes the work of critical academic scholars. It is a question of survival.[4] Therefore, it is important to remember that not all practices of critique are the same. Asking for forged passports, making forged passports, and crossing borders using forged passports are collective struggles through which people who are deprived of freedom of movement question the violent colonial and capitalist politics of movement.

If design is capable of such subversion, of being critical, then forgers should be thought as critical designers and forgery as critical designerly practice. Forgery is a critical designerly practice because, first, it facilitates functions, uses, or practical goals. Second, forgers and forgery reveal the hegemony of power: in this context, the mobility regime. Third, forged documents are not innocent, humanitarian, clean, elite products of awareness. They are not "speculative" at all. They are real, pragmatic products designed for a particular need, and they reproduce one type of market—irregular and less expensive— while disrupting other markets—legal and expensive. At the same time, their circulation in the regime of mobility evinces the vulnerability of sovereign power and hegemonic actors. A forger, who would not usually call herself or himself a critical designer, deserves to be thought of and discussed in a way that goes beyond his or her criminalization.

Forged passports do something positive and negative. The traveler might cross and apply for asylum and/or she or he might be arrested or be exploited by brokers. They achieve these opposing outcomes without falling into the trap of making the practice of critique a statement in a gallery, which is often the case in critical design.

A well-known approach to considering design a critical practice is expressed by Antohny Dune and Fiona Raby in *Design Noir* (2001). Their writing and the projects they present in the book are widely referred to as "critical design." This approach to critique in design is a series of design practices that challenge the conventional understanding of design as a commercial practice, reserved for corporate companies and brand identities. Critical design in this sense is able to propose another way of doing design, a way that has nothing to do with traditional problem-solving tasks or the "service providing" function, and therefore formulates the possibility of questioning through design. Critical design practitioners believe that what makes design omnipresent in everyday life might also give designers the ability to raise questions about engaging with design through speculative and future scenarios.

Critical design, while remaining critical of mainstream product design, never proposes or adds any sort of meaning to the act of critique itself. In this sense it is not a refusal but a passive affirmation of design. It looks "clean," "nice," and "minimal" and is enacted in safe environments, such as universities and galleries. In fact, critical design keeps the act or practice of critique within design discourse, and can therefore be criticized or discussed on the basis of designed artifacts rather than practices, performances, and interactions, or in the general the articulations the artifact might generate. In this sense, critical design dismisses the relations or situations that do not necessarily discuss the future of design or technology. This is exactly where critical design is unsuccessful. Its attempt to bring the designed device or artifact in as an important part of the act of critique ends up fetishizing critique in the skin of commodity. Therefore, the artifice-based practice of critique becomes the main feature of critical design to the extent that one thinks of it as quite indifferent to politics as a driving force of critique and materiality. As design researchers Luiza Prado de O. Martins and Pedro Vieira de Oliveira (2015) write in their critique of critical design, "The political sphere of critical design ends where the design profession ceases its responsibility, that is, at the moment a consumer product (or a prototype thereof as 'critical design') comes into being." To practice critique in design, which is not separated from the political understanding of history, the status quo, and the future, one should not think of critique as a category, approach, skill, or methodology but as the "very state of being of a practice" (Dilnot 2008: 177). The practice of critique, therefore, cannot be innocent. The idea of passport forgery as a critical practice can inform those who are interested in critical designerly practices. The practices of forgery and migration brokery teach us that criticalities generated by material means target material conditions that affect people, things, and institutions in a violent way. Thus, any practice of critique carried out by the manipulation of materials in an inherently material world carries some degree of violence. The question is, then, in what direction, toward which bodies, and in what time and space are these critical-material rearticulations taken, performed, and enacted.

The Violence of Material Critique

Forgery as one practice within migration brokery is not entirely liberating or counter-hegemonic. Those who have crossed borders irregularly and have had encounters with migration brokers know well that according to their class, ethnicity, sexual orientation, gender, or age they can be subject to exploitation, harassment, or mistreatment. It is true that migration brokery functions outside of the law, but through its function, it also makes other rules. To violate them can also cause harm. Thus, migration brokery is the interplay of legality and illegality. This is perhaps why Janet Roitman (2004) suggests that smuggling is illegal but licit.

On a hot day in the summer of 2014, I sat on a bench in downtown Athens to listen to Rahim, an Afghan refugee in transit. He told me about his activities as a middleman, and his time in prison in Athens. As soon as I left Rahim and walked away from the bench, a man ran after me and asked me to stop. I stopped and walked toward him. He approached me. We shook hands and he introduced himself as Abdullah from Kurdistan: "I was sitting next to you there and overheard your conversation. I wanted to tell you that these smugglers are like microbes. They are corrupted individuals, they are dangerous and ruin various lives including mine." Being stateless for twenty-five years, Abdullah told me the history of his statelessness in a short fifteen-minute conversation. He talked about how he had been abused by states and border guards but also by migration brokers and middlemen. He tried with four or five different brokers and was robbed every time, never having received any passports or being given access to any service that would enable him to cross to central Europe. Completely devastated by his experiences, he has lost his family throughout these years of transit and he believes that both migration brokers and states are responsible for his losses. When I asked him what I could do for him, he said:

> Perhaps nothing! I sleep in this park (pointing his hand across the street where we were standing) until I find a better shelter. I have lots of contacts in different European countries, look! (he showed me a booklet with contacts of his friends) but they cannot do anything either. What you can do is tell my story so the world knows what has happened to me and how I have been betrayed by the states, borders and these individuals who benefit from such discriminations.

We exchanged phone numbers and I promised to share his story in my writing. Abdullah reminded me that it is dangerous as well as unethical to romanticize and generalize forgery and migration brokery as mere critical practices. Many precarious lives are violated directly and indirectly through such practices, practices that are generated by borders in the first place. It is important, then, to discuss what violence means, and how and by whom its different forms are enacted and performed on individuals and collectives.

Benjamin (1978), in his very brief, but widely discussed, essay, "Critique of Violence," originally published in 1921, makes a distinction between two types of violence: divine violence and mythic violence.[5] Mythic violence turns out to be identical to all legal violence. Thus the task of divine violence is to destroy mythic violence:

> [I]f mythical violence is lawmaking, divine violence is law-destroying; if the former sets boundaries, the latter boundlessly destroys them; […] if the former is bloody, the latter is lethal without spilling blood. (297)

There are many interpretations of Benjamin's argument, most of which interpret it as advocating for "nonviolent violence" (Butler 2006; Critchley 2012). Simon Critchley particularly points to the complex relationship between violence and nonviolence and argues that an ethics and politics of nonviolence cannot exclude the possibility of acts of violence. If we are to break "the abolition of state power" (Benjamin 1978: 300) we need to think of politics as something to be conceivable outside of law. This is a call for "subjective violence against the objective violence of law, the police and the state" (Critchley 2012: 219). What these lines tell us is that violence is sometimes necessary to destroy the sacred image that states have created of themselves both historically and in the present day, even in secular periods (Asad 2015). Often, this law-destroying type of violence may come from the "lower" parts of society, not only targeting the state's sacred image but also those who enjoy and benefit from that sacred image through historical and material exploitation.

Passporting is a violent regime in itself. Its violence, however, is not visible to those who smoothly navigate the space and time of passporting and the mobility regime. Its violence is revealed to some degree to those privileged bodies once this regime is confronted with other violent practices, namely, forgery and migration brokery. The violence that forged passports generate, however, should be understood carefully, and for this, one needs to think of the practice of migration brokery in all its varieties, intentions, and complexities, since its violence happens in different forms and toward different bodies at the same time. Migration brokery violates the sacred image of the state, as Amir confirmed when he said that the Swedish state persecuted him not because he violated the law but because he violated the sacred image of the state in the eyes of the public. However, migration brokery also violates and exploits many precarious asylum seekers like Abdullah. Migration brokery generates violence at various levels toward different bodies: the state, borders, the authenticity of citizenship, and, sometimes, asylum seekers, border transgressors, and those trapped in transit countries. This is why migration brokerage's violence should be carefully thought through and framed around those acts of "profanation" (Agamben 2007) of the sacredness of the state, its boundaries, and its ultimate image as the only protector of people. It is in this sense that one can think of forgery as a form of nonviolent violence that promotes and mobilizes its violence against the state and the authenticity of citizenship, and at the same time restricts and stops its probable violence against those who are the victims of the nation-state making project.

Forged passports tell us that any material act of critique "costs" something. Any materially engaged critique that intervenes in a situation involves some sort of violence. Forged passports are part of an ambiguous space, operating outside or in between established, legal, normalized, and accepted spaces. They may be used for state-sponsored and non-state-sponsored terrorism and human trafficking but also for asylum seekers who flee war and invasion. Forged passports, like legal and official passports, play into an ambiguous field of power relations between individuals, states, and other actors. In order to utilize them critically and politically, one needs to contextualize them as situated practices of revolt, in relation to particular hegemonic points. This is how rearticulations and their "tendential combinations" (Hall 1996) become important in the discussion of design politics and its productions. Therefore, it is always important to discuss forgery in relation to the historical power relations in which it is situated and the power relations that it produces.

Abdullah's experience of migration brokers, which is not an exception and resonates with many others who have tried to transgress borders, points to a disagreement in the Marxist tradition of revolution. Marx and Engels would categorize migration brokers as the "lumpenproletariat," as "dangerous classes" (1848) who have no useful role in production, are unlikely to achieve class-consciousness, and are therefore of no use to revolutionary struggle. Marx, in *The 18th Brumaire of Louis Bonaparte* (1979), accuses the lumpenproletariat of being Louis Bonaparte's main powerbase, with this being the reason for Bonaparte placing himself above the proletariat and bourgeoisie. He describes the lumpenproletariat as:

Alongside decayed roués with dubious means of subsistence and of dubious origin, alongside ruined and adventurous offshoots of the bourgeoisie, were vagabonds, discharged soldiers, discharged jailbirds, escaped galley slaves, swindlers, mountebanks, lazzaroni, pickpockets, tricksters, gamblers, *maquereaux* [pimps], brothel keepers, porters, literati, organ grinders, ragpickers, knife grinders, tinkers, beggars—in short, the whole indefinite, disintegrated mass, thrown hither and thither, which the French call *la bohème*. (149)

Frantz Fanon, in *The Wretched of the Earth* (Fanon 1963), writing in the context of anti-colonial revolutions in African countries and in Algeria in particular, while inspired by Marxism, opposed this view of the lumpenproletariat. Fanon believed that colonized populations' potential for revolution could not only be understood through the traditional Marxist analysis of the urban proletariat and its position in industrial production. He argued that revolutionary movements in colonized countries could not exclude and ignore the lumpenproletariat, as it holds both counterrevolutionary and revolutionary potential:

The oppressor, […], is only too willing to exploit those characteristic flaws of the lumpenproletariat, namely its lack of political consciousness and ignorance. If this readily available human reserve is not immediately organized by the insurrection, it will join the colonialist troops as mercenaries. (87)

Amir Heidari's call to all migration brokers of the world to organize a mass movement of refugees across world borders without charging any border transgressor is in line with Fanon's strategy of mobilizing such forces in favor of the oppressed. This is important not only because some migration brokers have the power to exploit precarious individuals, but also because they can easily operate on the side of states and against migrants and travelers in need of passports. In October 2015, Amnesty International published evidence that Australian officials working as part of Operation Sovereign Borders in May 2015 paid six crewmembers, who had been taking sixty-five asylum seekers to New Zealand, USD 32,000 to take the people to Indonesia instead. The Australian authorities also provided maps showing the crew where to land in Indonesia. The report raised concerns that this was not an isolated case, and that not only was the state involved in trafficking but, crucially, it also directed it (Amnesty International 2015). Thus, it is important to understand the potential that resides in practices of forgery and migration brokery and include them in a critical discourse that addresses the material articulations of immobility. As design researchers, we first need to position such seemingly criminal activities as specific critical practices of making, different from those of critical design that are produced and carried out in Western academic environments. Moreover, it is important to mobilize and frame these efforts toward a collective struggle against the current hegemonic mobility regime while being attentive to the power relations that these practices are embedded in.

*

To go beyond the analysis of passports, how they emerge, and to what they give shape is to use my privilege as a researcher to frame passport forgery not only as an inspiration but as an existing force that affirms the possibility of practicing politics through artifacts and artifactual relations in places and moments that seem to be irrelevant to design or politics.

My main aim with this chapter was to further discuss the passport and its internal capacities in the rearticulation of relations and linkages between materials, bodies, practices, performances, and interactions. Forgery is one practice within the mobility regime that rearticulates these relations and creates relationships where they do not exist or are not recognized as existing. Forgery as a technical and affirmative practice of critique rearticulates the materialities of the world through a redistribution of the sensible. Its specific ways of translating and part-taking disrupt the flow and order of things within the mobility regime rather than sustaining them. My exploration of this was done as a way to extend an understanding of design politics and its operation beyond passporting and to forgery.

Forgers and border transgressors use and practice forgery in both meanings of the verb "to forge": (i) to create something strong and successful, to make relations that do not exist or are unanticipated, and (ii) to produce a fake copy or to imitate a document or artifact. The way forgery works is through both the fabrication and the articulation of artifacts and artifactual relations, as well as the behaviors expected from the artifact and those who use it. In this sense,

forgery is an activity shared by both authorized actors—for instance, the state—
as well as unauthorized actors—such as migration brokers—in the service of
two different groups. The state forges relations between bodies, nationalities,
and their positions in the mobility regime by articulating a specific product
for its citizens: the passport. The forger forges these existing relations through
forged passports for those who are left without a state, for non-citizens who
are in need of a recognizable position in the mobility regime. As Amir Heidari
put it:

> The world is a forged reality. Forgery is what the state does. The state is a
> forged entity in itself. If Sweden issues 9,000,000 passports to define a nation
> called Sweden, why can't I issue a hundred thousand passports to those who
> flee war, conflict and violence and are in urgent need of help and movement?
> Based on what moral position, am I a forger, a criminal and the state is not?
> What is forgery? Forging is an act of making something out of nothing. It
> is bringing to existence something unnatural and presents it as natural, like
> the state, like the borders made by the state. They are forged; they are made;
> they are unnatural things that look or make us believe that they are natural.
> Making borders is a form of forgery too. Now, you tell me who is the "big
> forger" here? The state or me?

Figure 6 Maryam Khatoon Molkara holds her passport while still a male, photographed at her home in Karaj city outside Tehran, 2010. Photo courtesy of Kaveh Kazemi.

Figure 7 "You notice that my passport is thicker …" (min: 0:53)—screenshot from the video "Pride of the passport"—taken from YouTube.

Figure 8 A collection of forged passports stacked at the Swedish National Forensic Centre (NFC), Linköping, Sweden, 2016. Photo courtesy of Alexander Mahmoud.

Figure 9 Intended writing powder used to discover hidden traces of writing or marks on a forged passport. Swedish National Forensic Centre (NFC), Linköping, Sweden, 2016. Photo courtesy of Alexander Mahmoud.

Figure 10 Stamps and materials used to produce forged passports displayed at the immigration bureau in Bangkok, after Thai police arrested a famous forger known as "The Doctor." A French Interpol official inspects the materials used to forge passport. February 10, 2016. Photo courtesy of Rungroj Yongrit/EPA.

The Design Politics

Throughout this project I was constantly asked a series of questions: Are passports a design problem? Does the analysis ask for the redesigning of passports? Would a new passport diminish borders or is it impossible for any passport, regardless of its design, the technology it uses, and its practices, to exist without borders? Do borders call for passports, or are they the products of passports and passporting practices?

This book, by focusing on passport as an articulation of different relations, practices, and performances, has shifted the focus from such questions, which come from an instrumental perspective on design and materiality, to questions of how the world is articulated through a series of material makings and how it can be disarticulated and rearticulated through the same capacity. This shift was necessary in order to discuss the complexities of passports and passporting in particular and design politics in general.

An Articulatory Practice

Passports function in their pluralities. Pluralities within passports are not the types or designs of different booklets produced by different governments; rather, they are the environments produced over time and in their intersections with other socio-material entities. The actual passport tells us that the object itself is capable of the production of realities beyond the intentions human beings have inscribed into it. The example of expired and hole-punched passports affirms this. At the same time, passports cannot fail to participate in the environments in which they are produced and the environments that they themselves produce. Such embodiment shows that passports are central devices in a regime that produces inequalities through intersecting and interacting with gender, race, and class as well as with technologies, devices, and designs. These associations produce practices that are local due to their materialities, yet promote global rationalities due to their commercial benefits by the circulations of technical norms they validate and their capacities of scalability. However, this is not an issue confined to passports.[1]

In my study of passports, passporting, and forgery I have tried to work my way around this question by developing the concept of design politics. The passport as a device and the complex environments of passporting are good examples of understanding how this works in a myriad of ways. If the assumption is that design is concerned with concrete problems "to be solved" in localities and through materials, makings and artifice; and if politics tends to deal with construction and "infrastructuring" of making regimes of senses—defining who takes what part and how ideologies are supposed to be translated from discursive level to materialized realities—passports and passporting affirm that there is no external force or distinction between design and politics in terms of one being only material and not political and the other being only social and not material. There is no design "and" politics; rather, there is design politics.

Design, then—or more accurately, the act of designing—was understood in this work as an articulatory practice of both material artifact such as a passport with its own technical and social components and the relations between various artifacts, sites, and spaces that operate within the mobility regime that is produced and sustained by it. This is to argue that the ontological condition of design is always about practices of articulations. As articulations do not happen in an empty place and time but in an already-articulated world, then what these articulations do is always already a simultaneous act of disarticulation and rearticulation.

In this sense, design as an activity that happens in the world and within its forces and relations is connected with how the materiality of the world can be rearticulated and reconfigured differently. Design is not the isolated act of solving problems or delivering services geared only toward the so-called end-users in relation to a specific market or a particular environment or function as the case of passport shows us. Designing as an articulatory practice points to the importance of decision, orientation, direction, and negotiation in design actions. Samer Akkach (2003: 324) points this out by drawing on the Arabic word for design:

> [T]asmɪm (design) … [in] current usage, however, seems to be based on tasmɪm as "determining," "making up one's mind" and "resolve" to follow up a matter. Thus in linguistic terms "design" is an act of determination, of sorting out possibilities, and of projecting a choice. It has little to do with problem-solving, the prevailing paradigm, as the designer (musammɪm) seems to encounter choices, not problems, and to engage in judging merits, not solving problems.

The modern use of the term *tasmɪm* in the Arabic-speaking world reveals the directionality that design actions must always take. This is quite opposed to Western-oriented education on design, where design is often construed as a set of skills, techniques, and qualities to solve a problem, a seemingly innocent term that refers to making things better in general. To think of designing as an articulatory practice is to think of it as a process of engagement with an act of judging that exposes a choice out of different possibilities. Then designing becomes a matter of decision and direction embodied in all things that humans bring into being.

This understanding of design in terms of material articulation is associated with an active environment in which design takes shape and participates in ecological, social, political, and economic contexts. Design in this sense can play the role of distributing senses and values, partitioning the divisions in society, from desires to labor and consumption behaviors. It is in this sense that the designed, designing, and the activities that flow from both are in fact political, and can be practices of specific politics. When, for instance, Jacques Rancière (2007: 91) talks about design as a configuration of divisions of communal space, he means the same thing:

> [B]y drawing lines, arranging words or distributing surfaces, one also designs divisions of communal space. It is the way in which, by assembling words or forms, people define […] certain configurations of what can be seen and what can be thought, certain forms of inhabiting the material world.

Therefore, design beyond an icon, symbol, identity, profession, or finished product is a certain mode of acting in the world that distributes, configures, and arranges social actions, sensual perceptions, and articulations of being together or being apart.

In this way, a design action is not a mere instruction embedded into products. Nor is a design action merely embedded in its interaction with the users or the environments and the ways it conducts the experience of use. Rather, design (in the three meanings of the term discussed in this book) should be understood as a dynamic articulatory practice that is historically and politically concerned with "what [the] action creates beyond what it instrumentally directed" (Fry 2009). To put it differently, design actions are those decisions and directions that take action, rather than acting on the basis of designed instructions. Design, due to its condition, is always a mode of acting, of doing and of configuring the situation in order to propose other possible situations. As Clive Dilnot (2005) writes:

> Essentially design is nothing else but the encounter with given realities (actualities, situations, circumstances, conditions or experiences) in terms of their transformative possibilities and potentialities. Design opens these possibilities through initiating a process of negotiation with the given which extends the boundaries of the previously possible. In so doing it transforms notions of actuality (unpaginated).

The call for a political understanding of design requires working with various design discourses and practices in a different manner. For this reason, this book as a work of "design studies" has moved beyond an isolated study of the design of objects, services, or systems irrespective of whether or not these objects, services, or systems are acknowledged by various institutions as design works. One of the main tasks of design studies is to question the "best practices" of design, which can ultimately change how design is carried out (Clark and Brody 2009: 2). This is why *The Design Politics of The Passport* aligned itself with the understanding of design studies that tries to discuss, unpack, negotiate, and practice the idea of design as a set of actions "to change the material history and practices of our societies" (Tonkinwise 2014: 31); an attempt that might give design in general and design studies in particular a coherence "that could resist the surge of capitalism toward this or that technological imperialism," (Tonkinwise 2014: 31) which is always fashioned through designerly products and systems.

The necessity to know and understand design as an inherently political action and an attempt to reorient its capacities toward certain directions is what the task of design, which is concerned with possible articulations of politics, could be. However these possibilities are not just there or given. There are always matters of orientations at work in any act of designing. In her lengthy exposition of this concept, Sara Ahmed (2006) understands orientations as arising as part of an ongoing history of things being specifically directed more in certain directions than others: "to orientate oneself by facing a direction is to participate in a longer history in which certain 'directions' are 'given to' certain places" (112). The passport situations exposed in this book have shown how objects shape bodies, politics of movement, and our understanding of who can be written and read as a legal body: as a "righteous" person in enacting her or his right to move. In this sense, it was an affirmation of how "bodies as well as objects take shape through being orientated toward each other" (54) and consequently render those orientations given and neutral.

This book as whole has aimed at exposing these orientations in order to challenge two main assumptions: (i) that artifacts do not possess or exemplify politics and (ii) that the apparent simplicity of designed things represents their essence. By examining the passport as one powerful material articulation of the current mobility regime, my aim was to show its emergence and design in specific moments and under certain circumstances. This helped me to expose how the production of illegalization and immobility has been accepted through material realities, through design and design's ontological power to orientate, persuade, normalize, and convince. Designed things such as passports do not come into existence through an isolated act of design or a single policy. Technologies, practices, and rationalities merge into each other through the act of designing. The act of designing articulates them into a new form seen and understood as a product, a service, or a system. These processes are presented and accepted in certain moments as principal components of modernity, capitalism, colonialism, and (neo)liberalism. Thus, by participating in certain directions, they come to orientate their positions in the world as a "natural" and self-evident bounded whole—which is designed, produced, and consumed in the name of reason and rationality—and as an indispensable part of the status quo.

Vulnerability of Design

While this book has showed that design should be understood beyond the actual product and its simplistic representations, there is a risk in locating the existence and operation of design in a more expanded field than what traditionally has been envisioned. I have argued for this understanding of design with the hope of locating the politics and violence of design beyond its interaction with its intended environment or end-users. At the same time, I am writing these lines in a discursive sphere, in which—commercial and corporate sectors of Silicon Valley to start-ups and NGOs to academic milieus and conferences—"the power of design," as a change agent is frequently praised, discussed, and funded. It is no surprise that a practice like design, which historically and institutionally has been part of the capitalist productions of norms and values, can be called in as an agent for promotion of neoliberal restructuring of the market and societies worldwide. Yet, one important difference in recent calls upon design is the ways in which it has been argued for tackling almost any existing contemporary challenges globally and locally.

One of the reasons for such advocacy is the ontological condition of design as it deals with imagined unlimited possibilities of articulating the materiality of the world. As a practice that shapes the artifice by looking forward, every designed thing for the simple reason that it is made can also be unmade and remade accordingly. However, far more importantly, the artifactuality of design states that change is the only possible condition for design to be practiced. While this is at first signals an unlimited practice of making, in reality it informs us that the artifice is limited. It is the shortcoming of the artifice, its very material essence that makes it subject to change and vulnerable to other forces, and consequently is always a limited possibility. And it is such limits that make design possible in the first place. It is due to the limitations of design that the limitations of the mobility regime are exposed by forgers and border transgressors, and in return, design is called upon again to redesign, to refine, and to improve the passport.

When I told the migration broker Amir Heidari that the new biometric passports are supposed to be really hard to forge and asked him how one might forge the information registered in data banks to be compared to the body carrying a forged passport, he replied that he knows that it has become harder to forge passports, to cross borders illegally, but he and others have shown that it is not impossible, and that migrants are the ones who have to pay a higher price for these securitizations:

> We always find other ways, techniques and methods that can get through these so-called walls and secure borders. In 2001, while I was in prison, my colleagues contacted me and informed me about newly designed passports. They told me that this one is really hard to forge. The information is not printed on paper or laminate but inscribed to the plastic surface of the first page. I asked them to send me one of the new ones so that during my time in prison I could figure out how to forge it. Once I started to work on the new one, manipulating the cover and scratching the surface smoothly, I realized how one could disassemble the passport and reassemble it with new information registered to it. We made it in a way that the criminal forensic lab in Sweden confirmed that it was impossible for the police to recognize the difference between the forged passport and the authentic one. However we made one mistake. The bundling and stitching of the forged passport was done in the opposite direction compared to the original one. But no police officer or border guard could find out this error.

Forgery as an act of redesigning shows the limitations of the mobility regime in mutually binding relationships. Passporting and forgery account for one another. While the authorities do not acknowledge the vulnerability of design by redesigning even more secured passports, forgers operate exactly through that vulnerability recognized. While one group such as commercial actors, lobbyists, and even academics who believe in unlimited potential of design, hides the limitations of design, others only believe in the vulnerability of design, in design as a limited and partial practice. As these material practices are never fully repeated and performed in the same way they are envisioned, their contingency makes them vulnerable to technical failures as well as interventions such as forgery.

Thus the limits of design are not necessarily a negative force. They are informing in many ways and they should be acknowledged. For instance, as it was discussed, citizenship as a conceptual and discursive phenomenon is actualized and made accessible through various material articulations, including passports. At the same time these material articulations pose serious challenges to the sacredness of the concept. Passports make citizenship vulnerable and citizenship cannot be enacted, accessed, and claimed without material articulations like passport. The point is not to solve this tension as states and security companies constantly trying to do so but rather to ask an important and urgent question: who has the agency to negotiate the tension and how? Travelers without the right papers by traveling with forged passport first expose such vulnerability that frequently hides itself behind newest technologies and, second, claim the negotiation over this tension however momentarily and modestly.

This is why a better design would not "solve" the issues raised in this book. When discussing design as an internal force in tackling various social, political, and environmental challenges, design cannot be the "only" response because it is limited by its history, practice, and reach in relation to those challenges. Moreover its ontological condition makes it vulnerable to eventual rearticulation. It can never be an agent of "massive change," a universal mode of intervention but rather of what Lucy Suchman (2011: 16) calls "modest interventions within ongoing, continually shifting and unfolding, landscapes of transformation."

Ethics of Design

In this book I have problematized the perspective that sees designing as a task of problem-solving or service-delivering and proposed earlier to see designing as an articulatory practice that helps us to be sensitive to its history, politics, and limits; to its orientations. By articulations, I refer to the acts of negotiation in forging certain relations that may or may not follow the tendential historical and material connections determined by strong forces of the mobility regime such as colonialism, imperialism, and capitalism. Once we begin to understand design and the position of the designer through articulatory practice, designers encounter choices to be made on the basis of the positions they occupy or have taken, rather than problems to be solved, services to be delivered, or improvements to be facilitated. This consequently locates designers' bodies and subjectivities in relation to the other bodies and subjectivities involved in any act of articulation.

This introduces another way of discussing ethics in and of design. The ethics of design can no longer be reduced to a set of moral and judgmental concerns as some sort of external feature to be implemented and achieved. By thinking of designed things as material articulations and designing as an articulatory practice, ethics become about recognizing the politics of the locations and conditions within which one works, and the politics that is generated from working within those conditions. Consequently, the relation of ethics to design is not a matter of "adding" ethics to design or making design ethical; it is about recognizing how design already contains ethical implications and being able to act on that recognition.

As it was shown, passports for many inhabitants of the world are part of devising their lived experiences and of how they experience the world. For many, however, this artifact still is an instrument that at best would satisfy their needs and speed up their pace of mobility when borders, border guards, and bodies are all connected to each other, as in the case of recent experiments with new smart border crossing initiatives in major airports of the Global North, for instance, in the Netherlands and Australia. Yet designers who are busy with connecting devices, networks, people, and environments in more and more user-friendly ways so rarely recognize the disconnections they design as a consequence of their promotion of interactivity and digitalization.

This book brought about stories of how movement across territories has been and still is regulated through the specific material and technical practice of designing, expanding, and sustaining passports. At the same time, it has been more of a project on immobilities as a particular design paradigm and practice. While there is much scholarship on how design facilitates, helps, and supports mobilities, this book looked at the other side of the spectrum and highlighted how bodies, subjectivities, and their possibilities to act in the world have been, are, and will continue to be immobilized by designed things and design activities.

When a new e-passport acts as the border and border guard simultaneously to reduce the time spent in passport check queues, for many this design is a way of smoothing their experience and interactions at the given checkpoints; therefore, they do not "feel" the border. But what these designs do is reducing our engagement with the world into limited and receptive measures that hide the politics of mobility regime exposed in this book. In this sense the seemingly most ethical designer, best attuned to the needs of users through human-centered approaches, "will generate the least ethical outcome, the one that most fully services others' needs, thereby disabling them" (Tonkinwise 2004) in understanding the design politics that is at work in any situation and context around materialities. In this regard, perhaps the unfinished, not completely user-friendly, and half-functional design is more ethical than its more effective counterparts. And this is why travelers without the right papers, those whose passports function partially and only after modification provided by forgery, can enact the ethics embedded in passports, the essential force of its materiality, better than the authentic owners, the citizens who carry one or more functional passports. A traveler without the right paper learns to engage with the materiality of the border politics precisely because she or he comes up against the materiality of its institutions and practices through their lack of a functioning and user-friendly passport; a device that paradoxically has hidden the materiality of the border politics behind a seemingly immaterial and seamless space of travel and mobility. As Ahmed (2017: 138) puts it: "If we are hit by something, we become conscious of something." Those who do not come up against the materiality of the mobility regime, against passporting, would not recognize the materiality of the right to move, and thus would not be able to enact the ethics embedded in the materiality of the world and its possibilities of access, movement, and residence. The first step in recognizing the ethics of design thus lies in recognizing the materiality of design, in recognizing its limits and its partiality in use for certain bodies.

The second step is to move from reflection, the prevailing paradigm in defining design activity, to recognition. This entails the recognition of the positions of designer(s) beyond institutional or professional ones.

Those who are fascinated by the actual design of passports and may participate in a new brief for a passport design that may represent their country or "nation" better, or make it more user-friendly for "everyone," are not necessarily crude nationalists. What they are unable to recognize is that the design of passports unites citizens in an unexpected way, despite the political disagreement among them. It is not that states consciously shape our perception of being, for instance, European, and then use different measures to legitimize this, rather that the European passport design shapes us as specific subjects of a particular imagined whole and gradually over time, through back-and-forth presence, gains significance. It is through "granting significance" (Bottici and Challand 2013) to a common narrative by a designed artifact like a passport that imagined communities such as Europe are produced and sustain themselves persuasively.[2] There is a smooth nationalism and racism embedded in processes of materializing citizenship via passports through modernism and its sense of technologically produced aesthetics.[3]

To recognize the orientations—history and politics—that identify the relations between objects and bodies as given and natural is to trace how certain historical forces have shaped the context of that specific design in order for it to exist and operate. In this book, the mobility regime as the context in which passports operate and become legible was identified. Consequently, it is impossible to ignore the fact that the current passport in our hands is a specific product of national, colonial, and late imperial ideas around mobility. Furthermore, like other specific material practices that have shaped colonial relationships, these designs are not bound to their specific moment and site of invention and use and move to other spaces once proven to be functional and profitable for the privileged. Thus, to recognize the paths designed things and design activities have taken to arrive to the present moment in which we rework, reshape, or rearticulate them is another aspect of recognizing why design demands an ethical engagement.

If design politics is about the articulation of materials on various levels and in certain directions, intervention in design politics is about disarticulating practices, performances, and interactions produced by the design politics, while rearticulating them in directions other than those taken so far or those toward which we are heading. But it is also important to remember that there is no formula for understanding design politics, nor are there specific criteria for making it. There are only moments, situations, devices, and things that can lead us to disarticulate and rearticulate possible ways of moving through, engaging with, and inhabiting in the world. Passports are one of them. There are many more to engage with.

Notes

Chapter 1

1 These investigations can be seen extensively in the work of Tony Fry (2010), Carl DiSalvo (2012), and Albena Yaneva (2017), who by using different theoretical frameworks concludes very different takes on the relations between design and politics. Tony Fry's trilogy on design, politics, and futuring and specifically *Design as Politics* (2010) places design as an inherently and ontologically political action that can potentially explore new configurations of politics required to address the unsustainable future we are facing. Fry builds his critique of the current forms of politics and design practice based on various works of political philosophy and argues for a move beyond instrumental treatment of design in and for politics. Carl DiSalvo (2012) rather gives a specific name to the interplay of design and politics. Drawing on Chantal Mouffe's works on "agonistic pluralism" and "the political," Adversarial design is the name given by him to a series of design practices within computational design that perform certain acts of agonism among human and non-human adversaries. However, by outlining conditions for political design in general and adversarial design in particular, DiSalvo gives adversarial design an important new role of political agency, as if the designed world of objects, services, relations, experiences, and things is not already political. Another recent work on the relation between design and politics is Alberta Yaneva's book on architecture and its potential for the political. Since Yaneva builds her main argument heavily based on Bruno Latour's work, she partly dismisses the subjectivities and histories involved in the process of making. For her, politics is not a matter of who makes things but how things come together.

2 I have borrowed this understanding of politics of design practice from the ways in which Judith Butler interprets Michel Foucault's ideas in relation to how subjectivity is formed within established domains of knowledge (Butler 2004a: 314).

Chapter 2

1 "Her Britannic Majesty's Secretary of State requests and requires in the Name
of Her Majesty all those whom it may concern to allow the bearer to pass freely
without let or hindrance, and to afford the bearer such assistance and protection as
may be necessary."

2 Gendered and racialized bodies as well as poor populations, depending on
different material conditions, were constantly seen as "unshaped others" whose
deceivability is in question. Simon Cole's history of fingerprinting (2001:
140–167) shows how expert debates on dactyloscopy were shaped by ideas
of the "indistinguishableness" of other races. For instance, in the context of
migration of Chinese workers into the United States in late nineteenth century,
Cole writes on the difficulties faced by authority to match the bodily description
on the passport with the body carrying it. In 1886 a representative of California
complaining about the vague written description of Chinese migrants' bodies
on papers doubted "whether even the most diligent clerks would be able to
compose truly distinguishing descriptions of an ethnic group so physically
homogeneous, in Western eyes, as the Chinese: 'there is a remarkable similarity
in the size, complexion, colour of eyes and hair, and general appearance of all
Chinamen coming to this country. It therefore happens that the present certificate
of identification issued to a departing Chinaman will do equally as good service
as a certificate of admission into the country for a thousand other Chinamen'
" (Cole 2001: 123). Similarly, Valentin Groebner (2007: 255) writes how in
medieval and early modern scholarly texts, women's bodies were discussed as
"unstable" and "impossible" to deceive because female body was perceived "'cold
and moist, thereby endowing [women] with the particular capacity to change
their appearance.' On account of such mutability, female bodies were described
as unreadable and literally indescribable—a topos that travelled from thirteenth-
century physiognomic tracts through humanist treatises on education to moralist
tracts on the depraved female inclination to paint their faces." For instance, in
1855, Carl Gustav Carus, a painter and psychologist, argued that women could not
really be recorded in physiognomic terms because "their exteriors are too polished
and their souls too soft and sensitive" (Groebner 2007: 256). Quite different but
within the same lines, practitioners of the Bertilloange of anthropometry often
complained about women's long hair because it obstructed their work on taking
accurate measurements of female suspects that complicated their identification
(Groebner 2007: 256). The logic of the indistinguishable other present in

identification practices throughout history has continued to shape the politics of identification at both a discursive and a technical level. (For instance, see Sankar 2001; Ajanac 2013; M'charek 2013.)

3   These ID cards (Kennkarte) were compulsory for three groups of German citizens: "German males from the age of 18; German nationals over 15 covered by the regulations for certain types of local border-crossing in frontier zones; and German Jews within three months of birth" (Caplan 2013: 231). Out of all these three groups, only Jews were required to carry these cards all the time and show them in all of their encounters with authorities. The ID cards issued to Jewish citizens had a red "J" sign on the cover and the inside left page. Caplan, citing archival materials from police ordinance in Berlin in August 1940, writes that the "J" sign was meant to mark a stigmatization and possible humiliation performed by authorities and even non-governmental actors such as sellers at train ticket desks in their daily interactions with Jews. For instance, this ordinance "describes in painful details at what point and what angle Jews were to hold the document as they entered a government office" (232).

4   There are conflicting historical accounts on the reasons behind the introduction of the "J" sign on German and Austrian Jewish citizens' passports. Sweden and Switzerland are thought to have been the main forces behind this idea. After the introduction of the Nuremberg Law in 1935 and the invasion of Austria in 1938, more and more Jews began to flee from Germany and Austria. The Swiss and Swedish governments felt that their countries could not take in all Jewish refugees, and therefore wanted to limit the possibility of their migration. They wished to distinguish those German and Austrian citizens who were coming to Sweden and Switzerland as tourists from those who intended to stay. The "J" sign was a method for turning away Jewish citizens at the Swedish and Swiss borders. In 1938 the German government began stamping the "J" sign on Jewish citizens' passports. However, during the war and from 1942 onward, the attitudes of both the Swedish and Swiss governments toward Jewish refugees changed for various reasons, and the ability of Jews to migrate to these countries was improved. (See Noll 2000.)

Chapter 3

1   The fascination in collecting expired and old passports beyond a romantic aspiration can be understood in this sense. For instance, see the interview with Neil Kaplan, a passport collector who unfolds the histories of Jewish population

displacement across Europe through researching stamps imprinted on old passports of Jewish refugees (Oatman-Standford 2015).

2   One such instance of romanticism is evident in the theories of Michael Hardt and Antonio Negri (2000). Hardt and Negri's romanticism derives from their dream of an autonomous movement defining the place proper to the multitude. Increasingly fewer passports or legal documents will be able to regulate our movements across borders. In their projection, a new geography is established by the multitude as the productive flow of bodies defines new rivers and ports. The cities of the earth will become at once great deposits of cooperating humanity and locomotives for circulation, temporary residences, and networks of the mass distribution of living humanity (396–397).

3   Heidegger (1962: 100–101) argues this by pointing to the fact that the object's very contours are designed with other entities in mind: "A covered railway platform takes account of bad weather; an installation for public lighting takes account of the darkness, or rather of specific changes in the presence or absence of daylight—the 'position of the sun.'"

4   This is not a mere metaphor. Today we know that the majority of countries and populations affected and displaced by the climate change are those that sit in the lowest parts of the passport index, countries of the Global South.

5   It is important to note that it is artificial infrastructures and material practices, for instance the system of passports, that produce social prescriptions such as fictional dichotomies of the pure and impure, the clean and polluted, rather than inscribing social structures into those artificial systems. It is obvious that social structures and political ideologies can be injected into artificial systems and artifacts, such as in the case of the New York parkways discussed by Langdon Winner (1980). We should nonetheless not ignore the power relations embedded within material things and practices from their very own positions, designs, and specificities as I am trying to argue for in this book. In his example, Longdon Winner argues that when Robert Moses began to redesign New York parkways from the 1920s to the 1970s, he made sure that the bridges giving access to beaches and recreational parks would be so low that buses could not pass under them. Since, at the time, blacks were not rich enough to own private cars, such parkways would automatically keep them away from accessing recreational spaces. As convincing as such line of argumentation may sound and it might be totally true of Moses's racist intentions, the problem is that it suggests the design or object is a mere passive medium that carries ideologies and does not speak back to the world in itself. Politics of passports should be recognized in

relation to their environments and their ability to move, to be enacted and to perform wherever they reside, which can produce unexpected results or/and uncertainties.

6   I remember when the reformist president of Iran, Seyyed Mohammad Khatami, came into power in 1997, he introduced a national program for producing National ID cards in order to replace the older identification system based on birth certificate booklets called *Shenasnameh*. As with many other reformists' programs, this plan was very well received by the national public, and the majority of Iranians (mostly middle class) considered it progress toward a more accurate organization of the population, referring to Western countries as examples of such systems. However, the production of National ID cards produced a hostile environment for undocumented Afghan migrants in Iran. Due to its design, the new ID card, compared to the booklet-type birth certificate, was made to be mobile and carried around in pockets. While carrying Shensanameh was uncommon and hard in practice, it became a norm and later a rule to keep an ID card with one at all times. Before the introduction of national ID cards, many Afghan undocumented migrants, due to their similarity in appearance with an "Iranian" national subject, could have claimed in their everyday encounters that they were Iranian citizens without materially proving it, since carrying a big booklet in one's pocket was neither common nor rational. With the new ID cards however, no reason was accepted. In fact, it was the design of new ID cards that first asked citizens to keep the cards in their pockets at all times. Later, the new cards asked authorities to find, arrest, and detain non-citizens through the absence of such cards. The new small ID cards for Iranians served as a progressive, unified, and Western organization of administration that smoothed many bureaucratic tasks in the country but also produced a new hostile environment for undocumented Afghans. One can argue that the government did not launch this program in order to arrest undocumented migrants—not only was it too expensive to be introduced for such reason alone but also the population of undocumented Afghans residing in the country at that time was fairly low compared to now. However the product in itself—the object and the possibilities and environments that it produced—could have turned any street corner into a hostile environment for Afghans.

7   Maryam's story has a double edge. She and her several years of struggle to get a religious decree from the Supreme Leader of the time have been discussed in queer and transgender scholarship in Middle East. She has often been represented as a pioneering activist who paved the way for other transgender

people in Iran to undergo SRS legally and even with the financial help of the government in some circumstances—to the degree that Tehran has become one of the SRS capitals in the world, despite Western understanding of Iran as a country ruled by a conservative and religious government that sees queerness and homosexuality as a crime. At the same time, many gay activists have argued that the way in which this religious decree was pursued by Maryam has turned the issue of homosexuality into a "sickness" or "disorder" that can be cured with surgery. Many Iranian gays have talked about the pressure from the government to undergo such surgery because being transsexual was the only way they could be recognized (Fayaz 2012). However scholars have critically reflected on how these two narratives collide with Western homonormative liberalism that always casts a country like Iran as backward in relation to sexuality. (For instance, see Najmabadi 2008; Bucar and Enke 2011.)

8   I am thankful to my friend, Amin Parsa, for pointing me to this story in relation to the passport.

9   The UK and Ireland have not followed the fingerprint regulations yet as of the date of writing of this book (2017).

10 Frontex, a European Union regulatory agency, is tasked with the integrated border security and fortification of the European Union's external border. Frontex manages operational cooperation at the external borders of the European Union's member states. Established in 2004 and located in Warsaw with financial, administrative, and legal autonomy, Frontex works to promote a "pan-European model of integrated border security."

11 In his work on governmentality, Foucault discusses the concept of self-regulation. By this, he talks not only about the "free interactions" of agents, entities, bodies, and things in the process of regulation and self-regulation, but also the production of a frame for these interactions to take place (Rose 1996).

12 Contrary to the positivist approach to interaction in interaction design literature, the conception of interaction contextualized here in relation to passports states that interaction is not an innocent or neutral concept. The interaction design literature typically treats interaction as a dynamic relation between humans and computational devices, digital material or environments, the quality of which can be enhanced or shaped (Smith 2007; Löwgren 2012) through deliberate acts of designing, inscribing interactions into one or more set of designed interfaces for work, play, and entertainment (Moggridge 2007; Sharp et al. 2007). In the more traditional understanding of the term, and within the Human-Computer Interactions (HCI) community, interaction is a designable quality between

humans and machines. This designable relation, which as interaction design scholars argue has apparently been dismissed by computer scientists, can be qualified and enhanced by the knowledge, method, and skills that design as a specific field and practice offers (Winograd et al. 1996; Löwgren and Stolterman 2004; Sharp et al. 2007). For many of these scholars, interaction design is not only about creating new things but also about shaping the possibilities of living in an artificial world, which is becoming increasingly digitalized. The justification for the emergence of interaction design as a discipline is a result of the growing interest in and importance of "interaction" and "interconnectedness." However, in a globalized, digital, and extremely technological context, one can read the story from another angle: we do not live in a world in which interactivity emerges as an inevitable part of the information age and digitalized ways of working and living, but rather one conditioned by interactivity as an economic and political commodity.

Chapter 4

1 It is important to note that while materialities and sensibilities are considered to be qualities, and part-taking and translating are considered to be practices, I will nonetheless show how all four different, yet interrelated, modes of reading and intervention are active agents in processes of articulation.
2 I use his real name because he wanted me to do so. Amir, unlike many other forgers and those active in facilitation of irregular mobility and migration, has always been open about his works and activities and consider this as a political position to be held.
3 After the Nazis took power in Germany, Walter Benjamin, a Jewish German philosopher, moved to France. In June 1940, when Benjamin was living still in Paris, Nazis occupied the town. He left Paris for the town of Lourdes one day before the occupation and obtained a visa to the United States two months later with the help of his friend, the philosopher Max Horkheimer. Then he left for Portugal in order to depart by boat from Lisbon to New York. Benjamin joined a group of Jewish refugees who crossed the French–Spanish border with forged papers. While in the Spanish town of Portbou, the Franco regime of Spain canceled all transit visas and the police informed Benjamin that he, along with the rest of the group, would be deported back to France. Knowing that deportation would only take him to a concentration camp, Benjamin committed suicide on September 25, 1940. The day

after, the refugee group that Benjamin was part of were allowed passage and they safely reached Lisbon on September 30. For a fictional account of the conditions of refugees and their experiences of border crossings, obtaining forged papers, or waiting for transit and exit visas in the southern shores of Europe in the late 1930s, see the novel *Transit* by Anna Seghers (2013).

4   This story is a retelling of a memory shared by the narrator in a reality TV program. To listen to the original in Farsi, see https://www.youtube.com/watch?v=S6gtWjrS0yo&t=244s, from 11:58 mins to 12:54 mins, published on April 15, 2011 (last accessed October 14, 2017).

Chapter 5

1   Of significant importance is Raoul Wallenberg, the Swedish diplomat in Hungary who managed to issue Swedish passports to Hungarian Jews and smuggle them out of Nazi-occupied territories to Sweden (see Noll 2000). Abdolhossein Sardari was also an Iranian diplomat in Paris who before the occupation of France by Nazis issued Iranian passports to Jews and helped them to flee to Iran (see Mokhtari 2011).

2   Because of the fact that as long as passports have existed, forgery has existed too, does not mean that the material conditions for intervention are the same. Passporting has become more and more lethal today and the technological conditions that keep redesigning passports keep reconfiguring our conditions of freedom as well. This is what a lifelong forger who helped Jews to leave Vichy France and later Algerian members of FLN against colonial French troops argues succinctly:

> Even if the techniques have progressively developed, forgeries will always exist. [...] A priori, everything is always possible. We must not forget that whatever one person has made, someone else can always remake it. [...] However, today, with all the digital technologies, electronic chips, biometrics, genetic fingerprints and card filing, I think there is no hope for people who need identity papers in order to survive. There are still little solutions left, such as copycats, taking over the identity of someone else, but it's all too fragile. Today, the Jews, Algerians, Greeks, South Americans etc., that I helped would be doomed, because forged papers can no longer be made "from scratch," as I did during that time. [...] It's no longer the same world. (Chamayou 2013)

3 This is what Rancière (1992: 62) means when he argues that the place of politics is that gap: "the place of a political subject is an interval or a gap: being together to the extent that we are in between—between names, identities, cultures, and so on" (62). The gap points to the contingency of politics wherein there is no "proper" place, time, or "proper" set of conditions for politics to happen.

4 A notable analogy between these two approaches of critique as practice is highlighted by Edward Said (2007) in an interview. In this interview, he compares Foucault's methods and knowledge production in *Madness and Civilization* (1988b [1964]) to Frantz Fanon's *The Wretched of the Earth* (2004 [1963]). While both works address issues of confinement, immobility, exclusion, and oppression where such violence toward subjects and bodies is justified in the name of reason and rationality-civilization, Fanon's critique is a "result of a collective struggle" and Foucault's is "evolved out of a different tradition, that of the individual scholar-researcher" (39). Both books were published in France in the 1960s. Unlike Foucault's, however, Fanon's book was banned one day after it was first published.

5 Many thinkers and scholars, despite being in disagreement over how one should discuss, understand, and resist violence, hold a common belief: that there are certain legal forms of violence which are frequently concealed as we are constantly told to identify only specific illegalized acts as violent (see Fanon 1963; Arendt 1970; Benjamin 1978; Derrida 1978; Butler 2004b). In his tracing of the theorization of the concept of violence, Idelber Avelar (2005) reviews the ways that "debates about legal or illegal, legitimate or illegitimate, just or unjust, 'real' or 'symbolic' forms of violence have been revived, with positions, as rule, being now more entrenched than ever."

Chapter 6

1 As Eugene Thacker and Alexander Galloway (2007: 67) have stated, "again and again, poetic, philosophical, and biological studies ask the same question: how does this 'intelligent,' global organization emerge from a myriad of local, 'dumb' interactions?"

2 A telling example of this is the recent passport for Serbia and Bosnia and Herzegovina. Both have followed European Union design protocol in designing their new biometric passports. However, in practice, these passports do not guarantee the same freedom of movement as other European Union's members. Nonetheless, the majority of the citizens of these two countries have happily

welcomed the new passport designs as an indication of their inclusion in European Union project.

3 In this analysis I borrow Victoria Hattam's notion of Imperial Design (2016). Hattam analyzes the fascinations with landing mats once used in the Vietnam War that are now being recycled for use in the construction of the US–Mexico border wall. Hattam argues that what makes these landing mats usable again is their aesthetics, particularly the forms of "grids" used in their design. Opposing an understanding of the state by James Scott, Hattam writes:

> For Scott, political authority shapes perception so that states impose grids to secure legibility. From my perspective, the most interesting political dynamics flow in the opposite direction; aesthetics bind us to state projects with which we might quite explicitly disagree. Rather than collapsing aesthetics and politics, I focus on the ways aesthetic attachments bind us politically in unexpected ways. Second, I am not replacing nationalism, whiteness, and settler colonialism with aesthetics. On the contrary, I am suggesting that aesthetics are one of the central vehicles through which these identifications get installed in us somatically. I find the mats beautiful not simply because I am a crude nationalist, rather, a nationalism is vested in me via a sense of modernism and its aesthetic principals. (36)

References

Abrahamian, A. A. (2015), *The Cosmopolites: The Coming of the Global Citizen*, New York: Columbia Global Reports.

Adey, P. (2008), "Airports, Mobility and the Calculative Architecture of Affective Control," *Geoforum*, 39 (1): 438–451.

Adey, P. (2009), "Facing Airport Security: Affect, Biopolitics, and the Preemptive Securitisation of the Mobile Body," *Environment and Planning D: Society and Space*, 27 (2): 274–295.

Agamben, G. (2007), *Profanations*, trans. J. Fort, New York: Zone Books.

Ahmed, S. (2006), *Queer Phenomenology: Orientations, Objects, Others*, Durham, NC: Duke University Press.

Ahmed, S. (2012), "A Willfulness Archive," *Theory & Event*, 15 (3).

Ahmed, S. (2014), *Willful Subjects*, Durham, NC: Duke University Press.

Ahmed, S. (2017), *Living a Feminist Life*, Durham, NC: Duke University Press.

Ajana, B. (2013), *Governing Through Biometrics: The Biopolitics of Identity*, New York: Palgrave Macmillan.

Akkach, S. (2003), "Design and the Question of Eurocentricity," *Design Philosophy Papers*, 1 (6): 321–326.

Akrich, M. (1992), "The Description of Technical Objects," in W. E. Bijker and J. Law (eds), *Shaping Technology/Building Society*, 205–224, Cambridge, MA: MIT Press.

Allincluded (2017), "Mali Refuses EU-Laissez-passers and Calls Airline Companies Not to Accept Them," *Allincluded.nl*. Available online: http://www.allincluded.nl/posts/le-mali-appele-compagnies-aeriennes-barrer-acces-aux-personnes-avec-laissez-passer-europeen/ (accessed October 2, 2017).

Amnesty International (2015), "By Hook or by Crook," ASA 12/2576/2015. Available online: https://www.amnesty.org/en/documents/ASA12/2576/2015/en/ (accessed October 2, 2017).

Amoore, L. (2011), "On the Line: Writing the Geography of the Virtual Border," *Political Geography*, 30 (2): 63–64.

Anderson, B. (2006), *Imagined Communities: Reflections on the Origin and Spread of Nationalism*, 2nd edn, London: Verso.

Andersson, R. (2016), "Hardwiring the Frontier? The Politics of Security Technology in Europe's 'Fight against Illegal Migration'," *Security dialogue*, 47 (1): 22–39.

Andrejevic, M. (2006), "Interactive (In) Security: The Participatory Promise of Ready. Gov," *Cultural Studies*, 20 (4–5): 441–458.

Arendt, H. (1970), *On Violence*, Boston, MA: Houghton Mifflin Harcourt.

Arendt, H. (1973), *The Origins of Totalitarianism*, Boston, MA: Houghton Mifflin Harcourt.

Asad, T. (2004), "Where Are the Margins of the State," in V. Das and D. Poole (eds), *Anthropology in the Margins of the State*, 279–288, New Delhi: Oxford University Press.

Asad, T. (2015), "Reflections on Violence, Law, and Humanitarianism," *Critical Inquiry*, 41 (2): 390–427.

Attfield, J. (2000), *Wild Things: The Material Culture of Everyday Life*, London: Berg Publishers.

Augé, M. (1995), *Non-places: Introduction to An Anthropology of Supermodernity*, London: Verso.

Avelar, I. (2005), *The Letter of Violence: Essays on Narrative, Ethics, and Politics*, New York: Palgrave Macmillan.

Baird, T. (2014), "The More You Look the Less You See," *Nordic Journal of Migration Research*, 4 (1): 3–10.

Balibar, E. (2002), *Politics and the Other Scene*, London: Verso.

Barad, K. (2007), *Meeting the Universe Halfway: Quantum Physics and the Entanglement of Matter and Meaning*, Durham, NC: Duke University Press.

Benjamin, W. (1969), "The Task of the Translator," in H. Arendt (ed.), trans. H. Zohn, *Illuminations: Essays and Reflections*, 69–82, New York: Schocken Books.

Benjamin, W. (1978), "Critique of Violence," in P. Demetz (ed.), trans. E. Jephcott, *Reflections: Essays, Aphorisms, Autobiographical Writings*, 277–300, New York: Schocken Books.

Bennett, J. (2004), "The Force of Things: Steps Toward an Ecology of Matter," *Political Theory*, 32 (3): 347–372.

Bigo, D. (2002), "Security and Immigration: Toward a Critique of the Governmentality of Unease," *Alternatives: Global, Local, Political*, 27 (1): 63–92.

Bigo, D. and E. Guild (2005), "Policing at a Distance: Schengen Visa Policies," in D. Bigo and E. Guild (eds), *Controlling Frontiers: Free Movement into and Within Europe*, 233–263, Farnham: Ashgate.

Bjerknes, G., P. Ehn and M. Kyng (1987), *Computers and Democracy: A Scandinavian Challenge*, Aldershot: Gower Publishing Ltd.

Bø, B. P. (1998), "The Use of Visa Requirements as a Regulatory Instrument for the Restriction of Migration," in A. Böcker, K. Groendendijk, T. Havinga and P. Minderhoud (eds), *Regulations of Migrations: International Experiences*, 191–204, Amsterdam: Het Spinhuis.

Bødker, S. (1996), "Creating Conditions for Participation: Conflicts and Resources in Systems Development," *Human-Computer Interaction*, 11 (3): 215–236.

Bogard, W. (2009), "Deleuze and Machines: A Politics of Technology?" in D. Savat and M. Poster (eds), *Deleuze and New Technology*, 15–31, Edinburgh: Edinburgh University Press.

Bonsiepe, G. (1999), *Interface: An Approach to Design*, Masstricht: Jan van Eyck Akademie.

Bottici, C. and B. Challand (2013), *Imagining Europe: Myth, Memory, and Identity*, Cambridge: Cambridge University Press.

Breckenridge, K. (2014), *Biometric State*, Cambridge: Cambridge University Press.

Breckenridge, K. and S. Szreter, eds (2012), *Registration and Recognition: Documenting the Person in World History*, Oxford: Oxford University Press.

Browne, S. (2012), "Everybody's Got a Little Light Under the Sun: Black Luminosity and the Visual Culture of Surveillance," *Cultural Studies*, 26 (4): 542–564.

Bucar, E. and A. Enke (2011), "Unlikely Sex Change Capitals of the World: Trinidad, United States, and Tehran, Iran, as Twin Yardsticks of Homonormative Liberalism," *Feminist Studies*, 37 (2): 301–328.

Burt, R. (2013), "Shelf-Life: Biopolitics, the New Media Archive, and 'Paperless' Persons," *New Formations: A Journal of Culture/Theory/Politics*, 78 (1): 22–45.

Butler, J. (1988), "Performative Acts and Gender Constitution: An Essay in Phenomenology and Feminist Theory," *Theatre Journal*, 40 (4): 519–531.

Butler, J. (2004a), "What Is Critique? An Essay on Foucault's Virtue," in S. Salih (ed.), *The Judith Butler Reader*, 302–322, Oxford: Blackwell.

Butler, J. (2004b), *Precarious Life: The Powers of Mourning and Violence*, London: Verso.

Butler, J. (2006), "Critique, Coercion, and Sacred Life in Benjamin's Critique of Violence," in H. de Vries and L. E. Sullivan (eds), *Public Theologies: Public Religion in a Post-Secular World*, 201–220, New York: Fordham University Press.

Caplan, J. (2001), "This or That Particular Person: Protocols of Identification in Nineteenth-century Europe," in J. Caplan and J. C. Torpey (eds), *Documenting Individual Identity: The Development of State Practices in the Modern World*, 49–66, Princeton, NJ: Princeton University Press.

Caplan, J. (2013), "'Ausweis Bitte!' Identity and Identification in Nazi Germany," in I. About, J. Brown, and G. Lonegran (eds), *Identification and Registration Practices in Transnational Perspective*, 224–242, New York: Palgrave Macmillan.

Caplan, J. and J. C. Torpey, eds (2001), *Documenting Individual Identity: The Development of State Practices in the Modern World*, Princeton, NJ: Princeton University Press.

Carrera, M. M. (2003), *Imagining Identity in New Spain: Race, Lineage, and the Colonial Body in Portraiture and Casta Paintings*, Austin: University of Texas Press.

Castel, R. (2003), *From Manual Workers to Wage Laborers: Transformation of the Social Question*, New Jersey: Transaction Publishers.

Çelik, Z. (1997), *Urban Forms and Colonial Confrontation: Algiers Under French Rule*, Berkeley: University of California Press.

Chamayou, G. (2013), "Fichte's Passport: A Philosophy of the Police," *Theory & Event*, 16 (2).

Clancy-Smith, J. A. (2012), *Mediterraneans: North Africa and Europe in an Age of Migration, c. 1800–1900*, Berkeley: University of California Press.

Clark, H. and D. Brody, eds (2009), *Design Studies: A Reader*, London: Berg Publishers.

Cole, S. (2001), *Suspect Identities: A History of Fingerprinting and Criminal Identification*, Cambridge, MA: Harvard University Press.

Crăciun, M. (2009), "Trading in Fake Brands, Self-creating as an Individual," in D. Miller (ed.), *Anthropology and the Individual: A Material Cultural Perspective*, 25–36, Oxford: Berg.

Critchley, S. (2012), *The Faith of the Faithless: Experiments in Political Theology*, London: Verso.

De Genova, N. (2005), *Working the Boundaries: Race, Space, and "Illegality" in Mexican Chicago*, Durham, NC: Duke University Press.

Deleuze, G. (1992), "Postscript on the Societies of Control," *October*, 59 (4): 3–7.

Derrida, J. (1978), *Writing and Difference*, Chicago: University of Chicago Press.

Derrida, J. (1988), *Limited Inc*, Evanston: Northwestern University Press.

Derrida, J. (2002), *Negotiations: Interventions and Interviews, 1971–2001*, Stanford, CA: Stanford University Press.

Derrida, J. (2005), *Paper Machine*, Stanford, CA: Stanford University Press.

Dilnot, C. (2005), "Ethics? Design?" in D. S. Fiedman, V. Margolin and S. Tigerman (eds), *The Archeworks Papers*, 1 (2), Chicago: Archeworks.

Dilnot, C. (2008), "The Critical in Design (Part One)," *Journal of Writing in Creative Practice*, 1 (2): 177–190.

Dilnot, C. (2014), "History, Design, Futures: Contending with What We Have Made," in C. Dilnot, T. Fry, and S. Stewart (eds), *Design and the Question of History*, London: Bloomsbury Academic.

DiSalvo, C. (2012), *Adversarial Design*, MA: The MIT Press.

Doty, R. L. (1996), *Imperial Encounters*, Minneapolis: University of Minnesota.

Douglas, M. (1966), *Purity and Danger: An Analysis of Concepts of Pollution and Taboo*, London: Routledge & Kegan Paul.

Dourish, P. (2001), *Where the Action Is: The Foundations of Embodied Interaction*, Cambridge, MA: MIT Press.

Downey, A. (2009), "Zones of Indistinction: Giorgio Agamben's 'Bare Life' and the Politics of Aesthetics," *Third Text*, 23 (2): 109–125.

Dreyfus, H. L. and P. Rabinow (1982), *Michel Foucault: Beyond Structuralism and Hermeneutics*, Chicago: University of Chicago Press.

Drucker, J. (2011), "Humanities Approaches to Interface Theory," *Culture Machine*, 12 (0): 1–20.

Dunne, A. and F. Raby (2001), *Design Noir: The Secret Life of Electronic Objects*, London: Springer.

Easterling, K. (2005), *Enduring Innocence: Global Architecture and Its Political Masquerades*, Cambridge, MA: MIT Press.

European Commission (2015), *EU Action Plan on Return: Communication from the Commission to the European Parliament and to the Council*, COM (2015) 453 final, 09 September. Available online: https://ec.europa.eu/home-affairs/sites/ homeaffairs/files/what-we-do/policies/european-agenda-migration/proposal- implementation-package/docs/communication_from_the_ec_to_ep_and_ council_-_eu_action_plan_on_return_en.pdf (accessed December 6, 2017).

Fahrmeir, A. (2001), "Governments and Forgers: Passports in Nineteenth-century Europe," in J. Caplan and J. C. Torpey (eds), *Documenting Individual Identity: The Development of State Practices in the Modern World*, 218–234, Princeton, NJ: Princeton University Press.

Fanon, F. (1963), *The Wretched of the Earth*, trans. R. Philcox, New York: Grove Press.

Fayaz, N. (2012), "Complicating Subjectivity and Transgression: An Analysis of the Queer Movement in the Islamic Republic of Iran," *Iranian Railroad for Queer Refugees*. Available online: http://english.irqr.net/2012/11/08/complicating- subjectivity-and-transgression-an-analysis-of-the-queer-movement-in-the- islamic-republic-of-iran/ (accessed December 6, 2017).

Feldman, G. (2005), "Essential Crises: A Performative Approach to Migrants, Minorities, and the European Nation-state," *Anthropological Quarterly*, 78 (1): 213–246.

Fichte, J. G. (2000), *Foundations of Natural Right*, ed. F. Neuhouser, trans. M. Baur, Cambridge: Cambridge University Press.

Fogg, B. J. (2002), *Persuasive Technology: Using Computers to Change What We Think and Do*, San Francisco: Morgan Kaufmann Publishers.

Fogg, B. J. (2009), "A Behavior Model for Persuasive Design," Paper Presented at *the 4th international Conference on Persuasive Technology*, ACM, Claremont, CA, USA, 27–32.

Forty, A. (1995), *Objects of Desire: Design and Society Since 1750*, London: Thames and Hudson.

Foucault, M. (1977), *Discipline and Punish: The Birth of the Prison*, trans. A. Sheridan, New York: Vintage.

Foucault, M. (1978), *The History of Sexuality, Vol. 1: An Introduction*, trans. R. Hurley, New York: Pantheon.

Foucault, M. (1988a), "Power and Sex: Discussion with Bernard-Henri Levy," in L. D. Kritsman (ed.), *Michel Foucault: Politics, Philosophy, Culture: Interviews and Other Writings: 1977–1984*, 110–124, London: Routledge.

Foucault, M. (1988b), *Madness and Civilization: A History of Insanity in the Age of Reason*, New York: Random House LLC.

Foucault, M. (1991), "Questions of Method," in G. Burchell, C. Gordon, and P. Miller (eds), *The Foucault Effect: Studies in Governmentality: With Two lectures by and An Interview with Michel Foucault*, 79–86, Chicago: University of Chicago Press.

Foucault, M. (1997), "What Is Critique?" in S. Lotringer (ed.), *The Politics of Truth*, 23–82, New York: Semiotext (e), MIT Press.

Foucault, M. (2003), *Society Must Be Defended: Lectures at the Collège de France, 1975–76*, ed. M. Bertan I and A. Fontana, trans. G. Burchell, New York: Picador.

Foucault, M. (2007), *Security, Territory, Population: Lectures at the Collège de France, 1977–1978*, ed. A. Davidson, trans. G. Burchell, Basingstoke: Palgrave Macmillan.

Foucault, M. (2014), *On the Government of the Living: Lectures at the Collège de France, 1979–1980*, ed. M. Senellart, trans. G. Burchell, Basingstoke: Palgrave Macmillan.

Freire, P. (1968), *Pedagogy of the Oppressed*, trans. M. Bergman Ramos, London: Bloomsbury Publishing.

Frontex: European Agency for the Management of Operational Cooperation at the External Borders of the Member States of the European Union (2010), *BIOPASS II: Automated Biometric Border Crossing Systems Based on Electronic Passports and Facial Recognition: RAPID and Smart Gate*. Warsaw: European Commission. Available online: http://frontex.europa.eu/assets/Publications/Research/Biopass_Study_II.pdf (accessed December 6, 2017).

Fry, T. (2009), *Design Futuring: Sustainability, Ethics and New Practice*, Oxford: Berg.

Fry, T. (2010), *Design as Politics*, Oxford: Berg.

Fry, T. (2015), "Whither Design/Whether History," in C. Dilnot, T. Fry, and S. Stewart (eds), *Design and the Question of History*, London: Bloomsbury Academic.

Galloway, A. R. and E. Thacker (2007), *The Exploit: A Theory of Networks*, Minneapolis: University of Minnesota Press.

Garret, J. J. (2000), "The Elements of User Experience." Available online: http://www.jjg.net/elements/pdf/elements.pdf (accessed December 6, 2017).

Gitelman, L. (2014), *Paper Knowledge: Toward a Media History of Documents*, Durham, NC: Duke University Press.

Glick Schiller, N. and N. B. Salazar (2013), "Regimes of Mobility Across the Globe," *Journal of Ethnic and Migration Studies*, 39 (2): 183–200.

Gregory, J. (2003), "Scandinavian Approaches to Participatory Design," *International Journal of Engineering Education*, 19 (1): 62–74.

Groebner, V. (2007), *Who Are You? Identification, Deception, and Surveillance in Early Modern Europe*, trans. M. Kyburz and J. Peck, Brooklyn, NY: Zone Books.

Groebner, V. and D. Serlin (2006), "Ready for Inspection: An Interview with Valentin Groebner," *Cabinet Magazine*, Issue 2, Summer 2006. Available online: http://cabinetmagazine.org/issues/22/serlin.php (accessed December 6, 2017).

Grossberg, L. and S. Hall (1986), "On Postmodernism and Articulation: An Interview with Stuart Hall," *Journal of Communication Inquiry*, 10 (2): 45–60.

Hall, R. (2015), *The Transparent Traveler: The Performance and Culture of Airport Security*, Durham, NC: Duke University Press.

Hall, S. (1996), "Race, Articulation, and Societies Structured in Dominance," in H. A. Baker Jr., M. Diawara, and R. D. Lindeborg (eds), *Black British Cultural Studies: A Reader*, 16–60, Chicago: University of Chicago Press.

Hansen, P. and S. Jonsson (2014), *Eurafrica: The Untold History of European Integration and Colonialism*, London: Bloomsbury Publishing.

Hardt, M. and A. Negri (2000), *Empire*, Cambridge, MA: Harvard University Press.

Hattam, V. (2016), "Imperial Designs: Remembering Vietnam at the US–Mexico Border Wall," *Memory Studies*, 9 (1): 27–47.

Hawley, K. (2007), "Beyond the Checkpoint," *Leadership Journal*, October 11. Available online: https://www.dhs.gov/journal/leadership/2007/10/beyond-checkpoint.html (accessed December 6, 2017).

Heidari, A., K. Ramqvist, and P. Wirtén (2005), "Är han Sveriges fiende?" *Arena*. Nummer 6. Stockholm, 12–17.

Heidegger, M. (1962), *Being and Time*, trans. J. Macquarrie and E. Robinson, Oxford: Blackwell.

Holmbäck, C. and M. Keshavarz (2016), "Passens förmedlare," *Re:public*. Nummer 39, Stockholm, 8–20.

Howarth, D. (2014), "Norwegian Travel Documents Given a Minimal Makeover," *Dezeen*, November 15. Available online: https://www.dezeen.com/2014/11/15/norway-passports-id-cards-neue-design-studio-redesign/ (accessed October 16, 2017).

Hull, M. (2012), "Document and Bureaucracy," *Annual Review of Anthropology*, 41: 251–267.

Ijsselsteijn, W., Y. de Kort, C. Midden, B. Eggen, and E. van den Hoven, eds (2006), *Persuasive Technology*, Proceeding of the First International Conference on Persuasive Technology for Human Well-Being, PERSUASIVE 2006, Eindhoven, The Netherlands, May 18–19.

Jansen, S. (2009), "After the Red Passport: Towards an Anthropology of the Everyday Geopolitics of Entrapment in the EU's 'Immediate Outside'," *Journal of the Royal Anthropological Institute*, 15 (4): 815–832.

Jonsson, S. (2008), *A Brief History of the Masses: Three Revolutions*, New York: Columbia University Press.

Justitiedepartementet (2015), *Missbruk av svenska pass: omfattning och åtgärdsförslag*. Justitiedepartementet, Regeringskansliet. Stockholm: Fritze.

Kannabiran, G. and M. G. Petersen (2010), "Politics at the Interface: A Foucauldian Power Analysis," *Proceedings of the 6th Nordic Conference on Human-Computer Interaction: Extending Boundaries*, ACM, New York, 695–698.

Kapoor, N. and K. Narkowicz (2017), "Unmaking Citizens: Passport Removals, Pre-emptive Policing and the Reimagining of Colonial Governmentalities", *Ethnic and Racial Studies*, DOI:10.1080/01419870.2017.1411965

Keshavarz, M. (2016), "Design-Politics: An Inquiry into Passports, Camps and Borders," PhD diss., Malmö University, Malmö.

Keshavarz, M. (2018), "Undesigning Borders: Urban Spaces of Borders and Counter-Practices of Looking," in G. Coombs, G. Sade and A. McNamara (eds), *Undesign: Critical Perspectives at the Intersection of Art and Design*, 161–174, London: Routledge.

Keshavarz, M. and R. Mazé (2013), "Design and Dissensus: Framing and Staging Participation in Design Research," *Design Philosophy Papers*, 11 (1): 7–29.

Khosravi, S. (2010), *The "Illegal" Traveller: An Auto-Ethnography of Borders*, Basingstoke: Palgrave Macmillan.

Kleinbard, E. D. (2011), "Stateless Income," *Florida Tax Review*, 11 (9): 699–770.

Korvensyrjä, A. (2017), "The Valletta Process and The Westphalian Imaginary of Migration Research," *Movement Journal*, 3 (1): 191–204.

Krasmann, S. (2010), "The Rights of Government: Torture and the Rule of Law," in U. Bröckling, S. Krasmann, and T. Lemke (eds), *Governmentality: Current Issues and Future Challenges*, 115–137, London: Routledge.

Krippendorff, K. (2005), *The Semantic Turn: A New Foundation for Design*, Boca Raton, Florida: CRC Press.

Kumar, A. (2000), *Passport Photos*, Berkeley: University of California Press.

Lake, M. and H. Reynolds (2008), *Drawing the Global Colour Line: White Men's Countries and the International Challenge of Racial Equality*, Cambridge: Cambridge University Press.

Latour, B. (1987), *Science in Action: How to Follow Scientists and Engineers Through Society*, Cambridge, MA: Harvard University Press.

Latour, B. (1992), "Where Are the Missing Masses? The Sociology of a Few Mundane Artifacts," in W. E. Bijker and J. Law (eds), *Shaping Technology/Building Society*, 225–258, Cambridge, MA: MIT Press.

Latour, B. (2007), *Reassembling the Social: An Introduction to Actor-Network Theory*, Oxford: Oxford University Press.

Laurel, B. and S. J. Mountford (1990), *The Art of Human-Computer Interface Design*, Boston, MA: Addison-Wesley Longman Publishing Co.

League of Nations Archive (2002), International Conferences. Available online: http://www.indiana.edu/~league/conferencedata.htm (accessed September 5, 2014).

Lisle, D. (2003), "Site Specific: Medi(t)ations at the Airport," in F. Debrix and C. Weber (eds), *Rituals of Mediation: International Politics and Social Meaning*, 3–29, Minneapolis: University of Minnesota Press.

Llach, D. C. (2015), "Software Comes to Matter: Toward a Material History of Computational Design," *Design Issues*, 31 (3): 41–54.

Lombardo, N. (2016), "Controlling Mobility and Regulation in Urban Space: Muslim Pilgrims to Mecca in Colonial Bombay, 1880–1914," *International Journal of Urban and Regional Research*, 40 (5): 983–999.

Long, N. (1999), "The Multiple Optic of Interface Analysis," *UNESCO Background Paper on Interface Analysis*. Available online: http://lanic.utexas.edu/project/etext/llilas/claspo/workingpapers/multipleoptic.pdf (accessed December 7, 2017).

Löwgren, J. (2012), "Interaction Design," *The Encyclopaedia of HCI*. Available online: http://www.interaction-design.org/encyclopedia/interaction_design.html (accessed December 7, 2017).

Löwgren, J. and E. Stolterman (2004), *Thoughtful Interaction Design: A Design Perspective on Information Technology*, Cambridge, MA: MIT Press.

Luibhéid, E. (2002), *Entry Denied: Controlling Sexuality at the Border*, Minneapolis: University of Minnesota Press.

Lyon, D., K. Ball, and K. Haggerty, eds (2012), *Routledge Handbook of Surveillance Studies*, London: Routledge.

M'charek, A. (2013), "Beyond Fact or Fiction: On the Materiality of Race in Practice," *Cultural Anthropology*, 28 (3): 420–442.

Malkki, L. H. (1995), *Purity and Exile: Violence, Memory and National Cosmology among Hutu Refugees in Tanzania*, Chicago: University of Chicago Press.

Martin, E. (2009), *Oxford Dictionary of Law*, 7th edn, London: Oxford.

Marx, K. (1979 [1985]), "The 18th Brumaire of Louis Bonaparte," in *Marx and Engels Collected Works, Vol. 11*, London: Lawrence & Wishart.

Marx, K. and F. Engels (1976 [1848]). "The Communist Manifesto," in *Marx and Engels Collected Works, Vol. 6*, London: Lawrence & Wishart.

McKeown, A. M. (2008), *Melancholy Order: Asian Migration and the Globalization of Borders*, New York: Columbia University Press.

Mehran, A. and A. Donkin (2004), *The Terminal Man*, London: Corgi Books.

Mezzadra, S. and B. Neilson (2013), *Border as Method, or, the Multiplication of Labor*, Durham, NC: Duke University Press.

Mitchell, T. (2006), "Society, Economy and the State Effect," in A. Sharma and A. Gupta (eds), *The Anthropology of the State: A Reader*, 169–186, Oxford: Blackwell Publishing.

Moggridge, B. (2007), *Designing Interactions*, Cambridge, MA: MIT Press.

Mokhtari, F. (2011), *In the Lion's Shadow: The Iranian Schindler and His Homeland in the Second World War*, Stroud: The History Press.

Molkara, M. K. (2006), "Tagheer-e-Jensiat Dar Iran (تغییر جنسیت در ایران)," B. Bolour (interviewer), BBC Persian, May 19, 2006. Available online: http://www.bbc.com/persian/arts/story/2006/05/060519_7thday_bs_transexual.shtml (accessed December 7, 2017).

Mongia, R. V. (1999), "Race, Nationality, Mobility: A History of the Passport," *Public Culture*, 11 (3): 527–555.

Mountz, A. (2011), "Specters at the Port of Entry: Understanding State Mobilities through an Ontology of Exclusion," *Mobilities*, 6 (3): 317–334.

Nagel, J. (2003), *Race, Ethnicity, and Sexuality: Intimate Intersections, Forbidden Frontiers*, New York: Oxford University Press.

Nail, T. (2016), *Theory of the Border*, Oxford: Oxford University Press.

Najmabadi, A. (2008), "Transing and Transpassing Across Sex-Gender Walls in Iran," *WSQ: Women's Studies Quarterly*, 36 (3): 23–42.

Navaro-Yashin, Y. (2007), "Make-Believe Papers, Legal Forms and the Counterfeit: Affective Interactions Between Documents and People in Britain and Cyprus," *Anthropological Theory*, 7 (1): 79–98.

Netz, R. (2010), *Barbed Wire: An Ecology of Modernity*, Middletown: Wesleyan University Press.

Noiriel, G. (1996), *The French Melting Pot: Immigration, Citizenship and National Identity*, Minneapolis: University of Minnesota Press.

Noll, G. (2000), *Negotiating Asylum: The EU Acquis, Extraterritorial Protection and the Common Market of Deflection*, Amsterdam: Martinus Nijhoff Publishers.

Oatman-Stanford, H. (2015), "The Politics of Prejudice: How Passports Rubber Stamp Our Indifference to Refugees," *Collectors Weekly*, December 8. Available online: https://www.collectorsweekly.com/articles/passports-rubber-stamp-our-indifference-to-refugees/ (accessed October 4, 2017).

Opitz, S. (2010), "Government Unlimited: The Security Dispositif of Illiberal Governmentality," in U. Bröckling, S. Krasmann, and T. Lemke (eds), *Governmentality: Current Issues and Future Challenges*, 93–114, London: Routledge.

Papadopoulos, D., N. Stephenson, and V. Tsianos (2008), *Escape Routes: Control and Subversion in the Twenty-First Century*, London: Pluto Press.

Prado de O, Martins, L. and P. Vieira de Oliveira (2015), "Futuristic Gizmos, Conservative Ideals: On (Speculative) Anachronistic Design." Modes of Criticism. Available online: http://modesofcriticism.org/futuristic-gizmos-conservative-ideals/ (accessed May 3, 2017), 61–66.

Puwar, N. (2003), *Space Invaders: Race, Gender and Bodies out of Place*, Oxford: Berg.

Rancière, J. (1992), "Politics, Identification, and Subjectivization," *October*, 61 (2): 58–64.

Rancière, J. (1999), *Disagreement: Politics and Philosophy*, trans. J. Rose, Minneapolis: University of Minnesota Press.

Rancière, J. (2006), *The Politics of Aesthetics: The Distribution of the Sensible*, trans. G. Rockhill, London: Continuum.

Rancière, J. (2007), *The Future of the Image*, trans. G. Elliott, London: Verso.

Rancière, J. (2010), *Chronicles of Consensual Times*, trans. S. Corcoran, London: Continuum.

Robertson, C. (2010), *The Passport in America: The History of a Document*, Oxford: Oxford University Press.

Roitman, J. (2004), "Productivity in the Margins: The Reconstitution of State Power in the Chad Basin," in V. Das and D. Poole (eds), *Anthropology in the Margins of the State*, 191–224, New Delhi: Oxford University Press.

Rose, N. (1996), *Inventing Our Selves: Psychology, Power, and Personhood*, Cambridge: Cambridge University Press.

Rose, N., P. O'Malley, and M. Valverde (2006), "Governmentality," *Annual Review of Law and Social Science*, 2 (1): 83–104.

Roy, H. (2016), "Paper Rights: The Emergence of Documentary Identities in Post-Colonial India, 1950–67," *South Asia: Journal of South Asian Studies*, 39 (2): 329–349.

Said, E. W. (2007), *Power, Politics, and Culture*, London: Bloomsbury.

Salter, M. B. (2003), *Rights of Passage: The Passport in International Relations*, Boulder, CO: Lynne Rienner Publishers.

Salter, M. B. (2004), "Passports, Mobility, and Security: How Smart Can the Border Be?" *International Studies Perspectives*, 5 (1): 71–91.

Salter, M. B. (2006), "The Global Visa Regime and the Political Technologies of the International Self: Borders, Bodies, Biopolitics," *Alternatives: Global, Local, Political*, 31 (2): 167–189.

Salter, M. B. (2008), *Politics at the Airport*, Minneapolis: University of Minnesota Press.

Salter, M. B. (2013), "To Make Move and Let Stop: Mobility and the Assemblage of Circulation," *Mobilities*, 8 (1): 7–19.

Salter, M. B. (2015), "Passport Photos," in M. B. Salter (ed.), *Making Things International: Circuits and Motion*, 18–35, Minneapolis, Minnesota University Press.

Sanchez, G. (2014), *Human Smuggling and Border Crossings*, London: Routledge.

Sankar, P. (2001), "DNA Typing: Galton's Eugenic Dream Realized," in J. Caplan and J. C. Torpey (eds), *Documenting Individual Identity: The Development of State Practices in the Modern World*, 273–290, Princeton, NJ: Princeton University Press.

Sayad, A. (2004), *The Suffering of the Immigrant*, trans. D. Macey, Cambridge: Polity.

Schön, D. A. (1983), *The Reflective Practitioner: How Professionals Think in Action*, New York: Basic Books.

Schwartz, H. (1998), *The Culture of the Copy: Striking Likenesses, Unreasonable Facsimiles*, New York: Zone Books.

Seghers, A. (2013), *Transit*, trans. M. Bettauer Dembo, New York: The New York Review of Books.

Sharp, H., Rogers, Y and Preece, J. (2007), *Interaction Design: Beyond Human-Computer Interaction*, 2nd edn, New York: John Wiley & Sons.

Sheller, M. and J. Urry (2006), "The New Mobilities Paradigm," *Environment and Planning A*, 38 (2): 207–226.

Simon, J. (2007), *Governing through Crime: How the War on Crime Transformed American Democracy and Created a Culture of Fear*, Oxford: Oxford University Press.

Singha, R. (2013), "The Great War and a 'Proper' Passport for the Colony: Border-Crossing in British India, c. 1882–1922," *The Indian Economic & Social History Review*, 50 (3): 289–315.

Skran, C. M. (1995), *Refugees in Inter-War Europe: The Emergence of a Regime*, Oxford: Clarendon Press Oxford.

Sloterdijk, P. (2009), *Terror from the Air*, Cambridge, MA: Semiotext(e); MIT Press.

Sloterdijk, P. (2011), *Bubbles: Spheres Volume I: Microspherology*, Cambridge, MA: Semiotext(e); MIT Press.

Smith, G. (2007), "What Is Interaction Design," in B. Moggridge (ed.), *Designing Interactions*, 8–19, Cambridge, MA: MIT Press.

Spivak, G. C. and S. Gunew (1990), "Questions of Multiculturalism," in S. Harasym (ed.), *The Post-Colonial Critic: Interviews, Strategies, Dialogues*, 59–66, London: Routledge.

Squire, V. (2014), "Desert 'Trash': Posthumanism, Border Struggles, and Humanitarian Politics," *Political Geography*, 39: 11–21.

Stanton, J. (2008), "ICAO and the Biometric RFID Passport: History and Analysis," in C. J. Benette and D. Lyon (eds), *Playing the Identity Card: Surveillance, Security and Identification in Global Perspective*, 253–267, London: Routledge.

Stoler, A. L. (2010), *Carnal Knowledge and Imperial Power: Race and the Intimate in Colonial Rule*, Berkeley: University of California Press.

Suchman, L. (2011), "Anthropological Relocations and the Limits of Design," *Annual Review of Anthropology*, 40 (11): 1–17.

Swedish Radio. (2013), "Är ditt pass köpt i Botkyrka?" "[Is your passport bought in Botkyrka?]" P3 Nyheter, March 01. Available online: http://sverigesradio.se/sida/artikel.aspx?programid=1646&artikel=5460272 (accessed February 22, 2016).

Thackara, J. (2005), *In the Bubble: Designing in a Complex World*, Cambridge, MA: MIT Press.

Thacker, E. (2013), "Dark Media," in A. Galloway, E. Thacker, and M. Wark (eds), *Excommunication: Three Inquiries in Media and Mediation*, 77–150, Chicago: University of Chicago Press.

Titchkosky, T. (2011), *The Question of Access: Disability, Space, Meaning*, Toronto: University of Toronto Press.

Tonkinwise, C. (2004), "Ethics by Design, or the Ethos of Things," *Design Philosophy Papers*, 2 (2): 129–144.

Tonkinwise, C. (2014), "Design Studies: What Is It Good For?," *Design and Culture*, 6 (1): 5–43.

Torpey, J. C. (2000), *The Invention of the Passport: Surveillance, Citizenship and the State*, Cambridge: Cambridge University Press.

Turner, J. (2014), "The Family Migration Visa in the History of Marriage Restrictions: Postcolonial Relations and the UK Border," *The British Journal of Politics & International Relations*, 17 (4): 623–643.

UNHCR (2017), Global Trends: Forced Displacement in 2017. Available online: http://www.unhcr.org/globaltrends2017 (accessed August 27, 2018).

van der Ploeg, I. (1999), "Written on the Body: Biometrics and Identity," *ACM SIGCAS Computers and Society*, 29 (1): 37–44.

van Liempt, I. (2007), "Human Smuggling: Types, Origins and Dynamics," in E. Berggren, B. Likić-Brborić, G. Toksöz, and N. Trimikliniotis (eds), *Irregular Migration, Informal Labour and Community: A Challenge for Europe*, 85–94, Maastricht: Shaker.

Verbeek, P. P. (2005), *What Things Do: Philosophical Reflections on Technology, Agency and Design*, Carlisle, PA: Penn State Press.

Walters, W. (2014), "Migration, Vehicles, and Politics: Three Theses on Viapolitics," *European Journal of Social Theory*, 18 (4): 469–488.

Walters, W. and D. Vanderlip (2015), "Electronic Passports," in M. B. Salter (ed.), *Making Things International 1: Circuits and Motion*, Minneapolis: University of Minnesota Press.

Warneke, S. (1996), "A Coastal 'Hedge of Laws': Passport Control in Early Modern England," Studies in Western Traditions Occasional Papers, No. 4, School of Arts, La Trobe University, Bendigo, Australia.

Weber, C. (1998), "Performative States," *Millennium: Journal of International Studies*, 27 (1): 77–95.

Wikileaks (2014), "CIA Assessment on Surviving Secondary Screening at Airports While Maintaining Cover." Available online: https://wikileaks.org/cia-travel/secondary-screening/page-1.html (accessed November 1, 2017).

Willis, A. M. (2006), "Ontological Designing," *Design Philosophy Papers*, 4 (2): 69–92.

Winner, L. (1980), "Do Artifacts Have Politics?" *Daedalus*, 121–136.

Winograd, T., J. Bennett, L. de Young, and B. Hartfield (1996), *Bringing Design to Software*, New York: ACM Press.

Yaneva, A. (2017), *Five Ways to Make Architecture Political: An Introduction to the Politics of Design Practice*, London: Bloomsbury Academics.

Index

www.ingramcontent.com/pod-product-compliance
Ingram Content Group UK Ltd.
Pitfield, Milton Keynes, MK11 3LW, UK
UKHW020702280225
455688UK00004B/218